ON
THE
BRINK

ON THE BRINK

AN INSIDER'S ACCOUNT OF HOW THE WHITE HOUSE COMPROMISED AMERICAN INTELLIGENCE

TYLER DRUMHELLER
WITH ELAINE MONAGHAN

A PHILIP TURNER BOOK

CARROLL & GRAF PUBLISHERS
NEW YORK

ON THE BRINK

An Insider's Account of How the White House Compromised American Intelligence

Carroll & Graf Publishers
A Philip Turner Book
An Imprint of Avalon Publishing Group, Inc.
245 West 17th Street, 11th Floor
New York, NY 10011

AVALON
publishing group incorporated

Interior design by Maria Fernandez
Printed in the United States of America
Distributed by Publishers Group West

ON
THE
BRINK

CONTENTS

INTRODUCTION

Vienna, Virginia. Summer 2005

T hree decades as a spy for the CIA put me under cover for years in Cold War Africa, in charge of the agency's biggest station after the Berlin Wall fell and at the helm of the European division, where I was responsible for dozens of stations and hundreds of people, at the toughest time in its history. Yet coming out into the light with this story has been one of the hardest things I've ever done. It went against the grain after spending half my life in anonymity in order to protect my identity, the safety of my family and the lives of my fellow intelligence officers and sources.

But so many misleading tales have been told about the CIA

since the September 11, 2001 attacks that after I retired in February 2005, I felt driven to set the record straight. One catalyst for this book was the unprecedented leak of the identity of Valerie Plame, an undercover intelligence officer, in an apparent bid to undermine her husband, Ambassador Joseph Wilson, a prominent critic of the Iraq War. While we do not know if there was any vindictive intent on the part of President Bush's administration to blow Plame's cover, at the time of writing, Karl Rove, the president's top adviser, is in jeopardy as a result of an investigation into who revealed her name and I. Lewis "Scooter" Libby, Dick Cheney's chief of staff, has resigned after being indicted on perjury and other charges in connection with the probe.

You will also find here uncomfortable details about the political machinations of the men surrounding Porter Goss, who replaced George Tenet as director of central intelligence (DCI) around the time I retired. I think it is important that the public knows the games that are being played with the agency at a time when this country needs a highly functioning intelligence community more than ever.

The CIA has always been a convenient lightning rod for the White House because its generals and foot soldiers are disinclined to come out to defend themselves. Like soldiers in a regular army, they feel it is their duty to serve—and even to die—and never to take credit for their successes.

I have grown increasingly angry at the way the CIA has been made a scapegoat for one foreign policy disaster after another. This tendency reached its most dangerous point with the September 11 attacks and the Iraq War, which heralded a frenzy of finger-pointing and emotional reforms that in my view will not help us achieve a safer world for future generations. If we do not face up to the fact that no CIA, under any leadership, will be able to supply the country with a silver bullet for the war on terrorism, or for any other foreign policy challenge, then we risk missing the real opportunities to improve our defenses against our enemies, be they suicide attackers armed with a few pounds of explosives or dictators with nuclear ambitions.

I want Americans to know that at the European division, on my orders and with the support of Tenet, we made real changes in the way we work with our allies abroad, the kind of behind-the-scenes earthquakes that need to happen if we are to prevent the bloodshed of Madrid and London being repeated in other capitals of the world. By necessity, these shake-ups did not hit the headlines. But they can happen and will continue to happen if we keep our eyes on the goal and politics out of the equation. The intelligence community must be allowed to do its work without being used as a political instrument, and real reforms must be undertaken. Tragically, we have once again imposed superficial fixes and purged the institution's memory with expulsions of senior officers, a trap that has caught us again and again since I joined the agency.

No president on my watch has had a spotless record when it comes to the CIA. Ronald Reagan used intelligence channels to try to exchange weapons for hostages. The first President Bush had a soft spot for the agency born of his days as the director in the early 1970s. But even he allowed officers to be pilloried for their roles in carrying out President Reagan's policies in Iran and Central America. In the end he pardoned those who faced the most serious charges, but this came only after a number of them had been pulled into court; still others, who had spent their lives serving their country, had their long and distinguished careers ruined. Bill Clinton took years to understand that the CIA could be used as a crucial instrument in securing peace in the world.

They all had their prejudices, where a cool-headed calculation of how the agency could best be used to serve the interests of the country and the wider world was called for.

But never have I seen the manipulation of intelligence that has played out since the second President Bush took office. As chief of Europe and one of a handful of geographical division chiefs in the Directorate of Operations—the covert branch of the agency—I had a front-row seat from which to observe the unprecedented drive for intelligence justifying the Iraq War and for someone to blame for the September 11 attacks. One of Tenet's most experienced top deputies, I watched my staff being shot down in flames as they tried to put forward their view that Saddam Hussein had no weapons of mass destruction. I watched as politicians, using intelligence that was at best questionable, spoke passionately about the impending threat of nuclear attack by Iraq before we sent our men and women out to die in the Middle East. I railed inwardly at the stubbornness of this country's leadership as it ignored voice after voice that warned of the perils of an ill-prepared war in the Arab world. Eventually I had to accept that nothing we said or did was going to change the administration's collective mind. Saddam certainly deserved to be overthrown, but I hated the way the public was told there were only two choices—unleash "shock and awe" on the evildoer or face the risk of nuclear attack from a boat in New York Harbor or a missile over London and more mass graves in Iraq. I reveal details here that demonstrate that there was another option available to us, one that might have saved American and Iraqi lives and made the world safer instead of more dangerous, as I believe it now is.

Now that I have retired, I am finally free to speak my mind in public.

While I could not include all the facts in these pages, you will find a missing piece of the story of the run-up to the war that will help explain why one ally in particular publicly opposed it so vehemently, despite being a country with which I have cooperated for years, with the enthusiastic support of our leadership. When I was called to testify before the Silberman-Robb Commission, which looked into intelligence failures for President Bush, I was questioned at length about this story, which relates to attempts by a close friend and colleague, who like other characters in this book, can only be identified by his first name, Bill, to make face-to-face contact with an Iraqi source to confirm his claim before the war that Saddam had no weapons of mass destruction. The tale of Bill's futile round-the-world odyssey, which at the time I foolishly believed might avert bloodshed but which fell like a tree in a forest in the rush to war, was not revealed explicitly in the commission's report. The commission believed that this issue fell outside their mandate, but it is an important story that should be told. Now you can read it for yourself.

It may suit this White House to have Americans believe a black-and-white version of reality—that it could have avoided the Iraq War if the CIA had only given it a true picture of Saddam's armaments. But the truth, as all CIA officers know, is always several shades of gray. The truth is that the White House, for a number of reasons, believed what it wanted to believe. As I describe in this book, the White House deliberately tried to draw a cloak over its own misjudgments by shining a light on ours. That is the kind of behavior that is guaranteed to prevent the agency from becoming the indispensable weapon I know it can be in the twenty-first-century war on terrorism.

In telling this story, I hope to continue to serve in the interests of the American people by giving them a truer understanding of the spies who work in their name at constant risk to themselves and to the foreign agents who are brave enough to join their fates to ours. It is very tempting, now that the Cold War is over, to say, as some CIA critics have, that we don't need the agency anymore. But in my view we need it like never before. I have run covert operations and undertaken them myself time after time and I know that we have skills that can be put to good use. Instead of running around frantically trying to figure out how to change our methods, we need to map out our targets painstakingly and patiently, as our enemies do, and get into the roots of militant organizations, as I know we can, because I did it myself when I penetrated the South African death squads and the African National Congress; and I saw our allies do it from my vantage point as one of the CIA's top operators in Europe.

We had begun in similar fashion to map out militant presences in Islamic communities in Europe when I left the agency, using the knowledge we accumulated unearthing spies before the Berlin Wall fell. That knowledge hasn't lost its usefulness with the passing of Soviet power, unless we believe that Islamic militants are driven by something demonic rather than by their own interests, and that their plans cannot be unraveled. We need desperately to apply our skills to modern threats, to tracking weapons of mass destruction and their constituent parts and identifying suicide bombers in the making. We have to work at this methodically, looking at local communities first. It is the only chance we have to stave off attacks like those that happened in Madrid and

London. Such random bombings will always pose the greatest danger, and we can never be sure of preventing them. But we improve our odds dramatically if we take the time to understand and cover the émigré communities from which they arise.

In revealing how politics and knee-jerk attacks on the intelligence community have prevented us from doing our best work in the past, I hope to reduce the risk that history will repeat itself in future. By speaking out, I hope to discourage politicians from abusing intelligence the way this administration has done, so that there is a better chance that a new, enthusiastic wave of professionals can be found to penetrate the madrassas, the mosques, and the Islamic centers where future Al Qaeda cells are being bred, to unearth sources and agents who might point us to the next Mohammed Atta or Osama bin Laden, in Europe and elsewhere.

So far the shake-up of our intelligence community that has quite correctly been undertaken by Congress has only repeated the mistakes of the past. It has purged and repackaged, but not truly reformed. There are new faces at headquarters, but there is no real reckoning with the events of the last few years—at least, none that I can detect. Changes were badly needed, but changes that would make the United States safer. The new structure is aimed at serving the requirements of the Washington bureaucracy, not the officers in the field and the analysts who must work without interference if there is any hope of really dealing with terrorism in the modern world.

At a time when we desperately need the brightest brains to go out into the world and find friends in unlikely places, I want potential recruits to know it is possible to do the job I love, to influence the policymakers by opening their ears to the truth instead of being used to tell a lie. I know because I have experienced it.

I could have kept my corner office with the view of the Virginia woods, after rising to the top of the agency, outranked by less than a handful of people. But it was clear I would have to kowtow to yet another series of new bosses as the latest purge at the agency played out, and I was past that. I fight my last intelligence battle in this book. I hope you find answers to some of the questions you may have had since the world turned upside down on 9/11.

—Tyler Drumheller
January 25, 2006

PROLOGUE

Vienna, Virginia. April 2005

T he day I first went public was otherwise unremarkable. The whole drama of my retirement, of the departures of my trusted friends and colleagues, of the arrival of the new CIA director, Porter Goss, of having to testify before one investigative panel after another, was behind me. So, too, were my nights of insomnia, the stress and exhaustion, the terrible unhappiness. I was looking forward to a new life in the private sector with the consultancy a few friends and I were busy setting up.

It was about 3 P.M., a Saturday, and I was at home with my wife and daughter. The phone rang. A reporter with the *Los Angeles*

Times was on the line. I had spent all my working life avoiding the media, escaping detection, and living a lie in order to serve my country. I had decided to write this book, but I hadn't really counted on making any headlines before I'd even put pen to paper. All I could think was, "How do I get out of the interview?"

The reporter, Greg Miller, asked me if I was the chief of the Europe division who was quoted in the final report of the Silberman-Robb Commission. The report revealed details of a telephone conversation I had had with George Tenet the night before Secretary of State Colin Powell's speech before the United Nations that justified the plan to invade Iraq. Without mentioning my name, the report delved into the other details of the debacle over "Curveball," the main Iraqi source for the claim that Saddam had weapons of mass destruction. I hesitated. I really didn't want to be cast in the role of whistle-blower. Tenet was my friend. The CIA was my life. The agency had been good to me. Even though my cover had officially been lifted in January, and I could legally tell people I had worked at the agency, I had not done so. Old habits die hard, and I still feel uncomfortable when "the CIA" comes up in conversation.

But then the reporter hooked me. "Just let me tell you what Tenet's been saying," he said. The next thing I knew I was hearing sections of a long statement issued by my former boss that amounted to an elaborate denial that he had received any warning of Curveball's unreliability. He also denied that I had mentioned the problems with this source on the telephone that night in February 2003. Here I was, being accused of not doing my job, of committing an "extraordinary lapse." Meanwhile, his former deputy, John McLaughlin, was saying he had "absolutely no recall" of our meeting in January 2003 at which I warned him about Curveball, even though there is a substantial amount of evidence backing up my version of events.

I was more disappointed than angry on hearing this feeble attempt at a bureaucratic defense. McLaughlin's response that day when I warned him about Curveball being unreliable had stuck in my head, and I revived it for the reporter, saying: "Oh my! I hope that's not true."

Finally, I lost my temper. "I don't give a damn what George Tenet says," I said. "He knows what the truth is."

What follows is the truth of what happened before and after that night in February 2003. We start where this challenging chapter of U.S. history begins: on 9/11.

Chapter One

DEADLY TURN

Langley, Virginia. September 11, 2001

After the planes hit New York and the Pentagon, everyone at the CIA assumed we might be next. It wasn't a stretch to think such a thing, as we evacuated and spilled outside that sunny fall morning, since Al Qaeda had planned to crash a plane into our headquarters in 1994. As thousands upon thousands of people tried to leave the premises simultaneously, a group of us, including the chief of Africa, stood and surveyed the jam of vehicles. I had started out my career in Africa and spent many years there; he too had devoted a chunk of his life to it. Mike Sulick, a Vietnam vet who was chief of Central Europe, joined us.

The chief of East Asia, a wiry guy who speaks fluent Chinese and had twice managed our affairs in Beijing, came rushing out of the office building and told us we needed to move it. A fourth aircraft had gone missing and we would be wise to assume it was coming our way. After all our collective close shaves, the paradox was clear.

"We've been through all this—Vietnam, Chad, Angola—and we're gonna die in the parking lot?" I muttered.

"Well, we could climb the fence," said Mike.

"I'd rather die," said my friend from Africa. He is a tall, beefy guy, and I don't suppose any of us was in such good shape that we could easily leap over anything, especially a twelve-foot barricade adorned with jagged metal. Still, it wasn't so much the physical effort that seemed unreasonable as the bizarre indignity of having to run for our lives, in our suits and sensible shoes, near the leafy, comfortable suburb of McLean, with its overpriced delicatessens, restaurants, and tennis clubs. That said, none of us celebrated when the missing plane slammed into the Pennsylvania countryside. We knew nothing would ever be the same again.

—-—

A couple of days after the attacks, Bob Deutch, the deputy chief of mission in Vienna, called. In Austria, we had spent a lot of time trying to devise ways to unearth terrorists in Europe.

"I just have to ask you," he said. "Did we do everything we could to stop this?"

I tried to reassure him, but it was cold comfort. "Yeah, Bob. Everybody feels the same way. But it happened because it happened." It wasn't the kind of thing that many government officials said out loud, but it was the truth. It's not that there was no chance we could have prevented the attacks. But the harsh reality is that even if you do everything right, you still might not stop a suicide bomber. Even Israel, with all its security and vigilance, cannot always prevent such attacks. In London, a second wave of bloodshed in the Underground was only averted because the bombs failed to go off, yet Britain, a small island, has one of the most sophisticated systems of surveillance cameras in the world. With the benefit of hindsight, it is possible to identify moments when law enforcement and the CIA failed to share information or spot alarm bells and connect dots in the September 11 plot. If the FBI had picked up on the plotters training in flight schools, if we had alerted the FBI about two of the hijackers arriving on U.S. soil from Indonesia, then perhaps we would have disrupted the plot. But we may only have delayed it. Arresting some of the plotters would not have revealed the full extent of the plan to us, since the attackers were pretty well compartmentalized. It is unclear whether many of the hijackers even knew what was going to happen that terrible day. That doesn't mean you throw your hands up in the air and say there's nothing to be done. We have to be vigilant and keep track in communities where suicide bombers may be waiting to pounce. But at the same time we have to be honest and accept that sometimes we cannot prevent such attacks from happening, instead of pretending that we can wipe terrorism out completely.

September 11 was a freak attack, a perfect storm. I remembered Ahmed Ressam, the Algerian who wanted to leave his homicidal mark on the millennium by setting off a bomb at Los Angeles International Airport. Thanks to a mixture of vigilance and luck, a Canadian border guard opened the trunk of the would-be assassin and discovered a load of explosives. Attentiveness like this increases the odds against disaster, but it will never rule out all attacks. Still, the chances of another attack on the scale of 9/11 happening are extremely slim. The bloodshed should have prompted an honest review of how we run our foreign policy and law enforcement. Instead of taking a long, sober look at those issues, the Bush administration put the country in a state of prolonged panic.

--

We were all afraid, really afraid, back then. My daughter, Livy, loves New York, and she was traumatized. To this day, she and my wife, Linda, make regular trips to Manhattan, and that week, Livy gave me a photograph of the Twin Towers and told me to put it up in my office. I did so without resistance, even though I'm not one for emotional flourishes. Until I retired, it hung in my office next to a sketch of a Lipizzaner, a painting of the cathedral in Vienna given to me by the Austrian service and a watercolor of fishermen on the North Sea coast. Unlike some of my colleagues, I had no "me" wall. Like many of the old guard who had spent years in anonymity, it felt weird to me—and feels weird to this day—to advertise any facts about myself.

I would sit there and see that picture of the Twin Towers and ask myself if I was being irresponsible by staying in Washington, D.C. Cofer Black, my first boss in the field and a longtime friend and colleague, had me convinced that Al Qaeda was going to fly over a plane carrying anthrax or come up with some other terrible way to attack Washington and New York again. As head of the CIA's

Counterterrorist Center, his views carried weight, and he was far from alone in predicting catastrophe. The whole administration seemed to hold this view. The assessment was based largely on documents captured in Afghanistan that demonstrated an intent to launch more attacks—but not that Al Qaeda had the ability to actually carry them out. But in the light of 9/11, the administration treated this wish list as a concrete threat.

In early October, Cofer had his first opportunity to update the Directorate of Operations, the clandestine branch of the agency whose European division I ran. He addressed the first staff meeting of my immediate boss, Jim Pavitt, who ran the directorate and had worked alongside me in the 1980s when he'd run the eastern branch of Africa and I had led the southern branch. We discussed how we would change our staffing plans and the need to shift resources from Europe to the Counterterrorist Center and so on. Cofer said he believed we were under imminent threat of several other attacks of a magnitude similar to or greater than 9/11. As my superior on my first foreign assignment, to Africa, he had been a colorful and energetic member of the older generation, and I had looked up to him in many ways. Adventurous and good-hearted, he modeled himself on the old-time agency officers and always bravely volunteered for the toughest and most dangerous postings.

The fear at the time reached right to the top of the agency. I remember Tenet, a man I've known for twenty years, asking me how my family was. I mentioned that they were planning to visit New York. He said, "Tell them not to go." It was an unusual thing to say at the time, given that the official line was for everyone to go on as normal. But at that moment, he was speaking as my friend. The atmosphere was stifling. Everyone was so convinced that New York might be attacked again that police were being issued with the equipment used in nuclear plants to measure radiation. Still, I guess I can't have taken the dire predictions too seriously, because Linda and Livy went to New York anyway. But I can't say I wasn't worried. I don't think any of us was thinking entirely clearly back then.

— —

It felt like years had passed since we'd returned from Europe, three months before the attacks. I'd felt back then that I was on an upward curve—I'd been promoted to the senior service at the unusually young age of forty-five, with more than twenty-five years under my belt. I was now fifty. I had done everything I could to be where I wanted to be, but I knew it was down to blind luck whether I advanced any further. I couldn't work any harder or get any smarter.

When I took over as chief of Europe on July 9, 2001, I was happy to be back on home turf. I planned to stay around for another five years or so, until I was fifty-five, and if another interesting job didn't come up, say at the National Security Council or at a more senior level at the CIA, I'd think about moving on. Having run the European segment of the clandestine branch, I didn't want to become one of those guys who just moved from running one division to the next, applying the same skills over and over to different areas. That could be a velvet coffin. I wanted to try new things. I had avoided getting stuck in a rut when I'd decided to move to Europe instead of continuing to serve in Africa, where I had established an excellent track record. Now I imagined I might do a teaching rotation at a university if I didn't get a more senior job. One thing I knew was that I wasn't sticking around until I was sixty-five.

I got along well with Tenet. We first crossed paths in the 1980s, when he worked on the Senate Select Committee on Intelligence and we both attended a briefing on Africa. (Although I doubt if he remembered such a little fish.) The first time I met him properly was in 1995, when he was deputy chief of the CIA and I was taken in to brief him after meeting a sensitive agent. I had had a break-through in a case that was producing real intelligence with a sig-nificant impact on security policy and on the agency as a whole. It had involved a lot of hard work over two years, with some resist-ance within the organization. Many individuals had taken risks, and I had traveled extensively in alias in order to pull it off. Tenet was always anxious to ensure that officers understood that their bosses valued their input, even if their victories could not be pub-licized. "I wish I had five hundred more guys like you," he said. I remember thinking that he was a good leader.

I eventually came to think of him as a friend. When we passed in the corridor at CIA headquarters in Langley, Virginia, we would stop for a chat about football or basketball. He was a great fan of his alma mater, Georgetown University, where I had also taken graduate courses, and we would discuss the fortunes of the teams.

In 1996, after I had become deputy chief of Europe, Tenet asked me to come on up and tell him what was happening on my patch. He was good that way, always keeping his ear close to the ground. He was also very close to John Deutch, the CIA chief at the time, who had elevated him from a position as special assistant to Bill Clinton at the National Security Council when he made him his deputy in 1995. Tenet had previously been staff director of the Senate intelligence committee and was really a political operator rather than an intelligence figure. Nonetheless, he was widely admired by many at the agency, including myself. The same could not be said of Deutch, however. After meeting him just after his appointment in 1995, I left with the impression that he was a truly intelligent man and that he could make real changes at the agency. But he quickly revealed a certain arrogance, and annoyed a lot of people by suggesting that Pentagon intelligence officers were smarter than the officers in his own building. He tried to retract the remarks, but the damage was done.

As I went up to see Tenet, Deutch suddenly walked in from the adjoining office, wearing a white dress shirt and boxer shorts, long black socks with garters, and carrying a squash racquet. He was a big squash player and he was getting changed for a game. He looked through the door and said: "The chief of Europe has a good deputy; mine's not worth a damn." After he left, Tenet said: "No matter what you think, I don't get paid enough." He was kidding, because they were really very close. The exchange was harmless, if rather inappropriate; a bout of locker room humor. But I certainly felt uncomfortable seeing my boss's boss in his underwear. Deutch had a way of making people feel that way. He would always ask where one had gone to school, and seemed to draw conclusions from the answer. I never liked that.

After becoming director of central intelligence (DCI) in December 1996, Tenet took a lot of criticism for not being harder on Deutch. Security inspections at his home and a subsequent investigation later revealed that Deutch had stored extremely sensitive secrets on a home computer that was also used by a member of his family to access pornography sites and send e-mails, activities that could make the computer vulnerable to outside interference. Tenet withdrew Deutch's security clearance in August 1999, and was criticized for failing to act sooner. Deutch, meanwhile, seemed extremely reluctant to admit his error, which to me just confirmed his arrogance.

——

As I got my feet under the table at Langley, senior members of my team arrived and we began to revamp the division to concentrate more on unearthing terrorists and weapons proliferation networks in Europe. We knew an attack might be on the way. Shortly after my arrival in Washington, an officer who had trained with me and worked beside me in Africa and Europe before becoming the chief of the Osama bin Laden task force told me they were worried about attacks in Europe or the Gulf, or even in the United States.

Cofer Black told me Tenet was furiously trying to get the administration to focus on the issue. As has since been revealed by the September 11 commission, which examined the run-up to the attacks, Bush was specifically warned of a possible attack in an item on Tenet's daily briefing of August 6, 2001, which was entitled: "Bin Laden Determined to Strike in US." The briefing also spoke of FBI awareness of "patterns of suspicious activity consistent with preparations for hijackings or other types of attacks, including recent surveillance of federal buildings in New York." The agency had warned top officials that Bin Laden operatives were expecting imminent attacks that would have "dramatic consequences of catastrophic proportions," as the report found.

As the weeks passed and the disaster approached, I met representatives from several European services, and it was clear they were more interested in organized crime and illegal immigration than in terrorist threats. My European friends, having lived through the Red Terror of the 1960s and 1970s, seemed to take a more sanguine approach to the possibility of random violence. As chief of Europe, with hundreds of people under my command at Langley and hundreds more at stations in Europe and elsewhere, I saw this difference in approach as an opportunity to leave my mark. I was devoted to the strategy of exploiting European fears of right-wing fanaticism to get our allies to help build counterterrorist efforts against militant Islam. It was a way to bring us to the same target. The Europeans had concentrated their resources on fascist groups who have had wider success there than they have here. My point to my European counterparts, again and again, was that they would help themselves by shifting some resources to Islamic militants, because if they succeeded in carrying out attacks, Europe ran the risk of seeing a rabid reaction from its right-wing fringe groups, which have won recruits by railing against immigration, a highly emotional issue in many European countries. It's not that the Europeans disagreed with this point, but it was an issue that I keenly wanted to focus on, and it was discussed when the heads of the European services came through Washington after Bush was elected and in the run-up to 9/11.

This approach remains highly relevant today, especially in light of the bombings in London, where the risk of fueling fascism was high if the response was not handled sensitively, as the British government seemed to do. One of their first responses after the bombs ripped through the London Underground was to send extra police to Muslim neighborhoods to prevent retaliatory attacks.

I remember, in the mid-1960s, when I was living in Wiesbaden as my father served in the air force, leftist radicals blowing up cars at American military housing installations. They were just part of a wider pattern of attacks that continued for years and grew far more severe in the 1970s. But there was never the kind of reaction there that we have seen in this country. Europeans almost seem to see terrorism as a force of nature, something that can be managed and minimized but never stamped out. And that is still the attitude in the UK despite the London attacks. The first response was to rush to get back to work, not to head for the hills. In Madrid, after the train bombings, the government did not start telling people to buy duct tape in case of a biological attack. The people elected a new government that pulled its troops out of Iraq, but there was no hysteria about the threat. The British set out to address the problem in tangible ways after the London bombs but did not set the country on edge. There was a tragic mistake, of course, when London police shot an innocent Brazilian electrician dead, apparently believing he was about to set off a bomb because he ignored their orders to stop. But there was nothing panicked about their act. They shot him five times in the head, as they had apparently been ordered to do if they believed another bomb was about to be set off. It was a deliberate, if erroneous, attempt to prevent more bloodshed.

But around the time of the 9/11 attacks, from the perspective of the Europeans, Islamic extremism was an American problem, and, to a lesser extent, a British one, a consequence of our close ties to Israel and conservative governments in the Middle East, especially Saudi Arabia.

This message came through loud and clear even after the attacks in New York and Washington. At a Christmas party in 2002, the head of one European service said to a colleague's wife: "You Americans are the problem. You're bringing terrorism to Europe by antagonizing all these people . . . we know how to handle this." At the time, I was almost relieved to see the reporting come back to Langley on this exchange. It was the message I had been trying to get across in Washington for some time. The Bush administration seemed to think that the Europeans were either too afraid of terrorists to deal with them or too accommodating in an attempt to keep Islamic populations happy. In fact, they blamed us for the emergence of the problem. Agree or disagree, it was important that the administration know this, so they could address the dissonance between us and tackle the threat in Europe, country by country.

The Europeans always said they would work with us, however, and generally they did. I thought it was a waste of time to beat them up, as the administration has done in recent years. It would have been far more productive just to collaborate and maintain a cooperative atmosphere.

In August, two or three weeks before the attacks, I had my first big meeting with my bosses in the Directorate of Operations. We agreed we needed to press harder on counterterrorism and counterproliferation issues in Europe. I said I wanted to be more aggressive, get the Europeans involved and find a way to work around their opposition to violating privacy laws without making ourselves completely unpalatable. My bosses were happy with that emphasis, and we agreed to move forward in that direction. But we had a struggle to sustain that approach given the emphasis of the Bush administration, which was to persuade

Europeans to change their laws to make it easier to detain people. It is much easier to get permission for a telephone tap in this country, for example, than it is in Germany, where you have to go before a committee of parliament. At the agency, where we are accustomed to finding more subtle ways to work with our allies, we know there are always ways around these issues if you approach the issue sensitively. In any event, bullying them to weaken their privacy laws was an unnecessary pursuit in the aftermath of 9/11, as our European friends needed no reminding of the importance of focusing on terrorism and nonproliferation. We knew pretty early on that some of the hijackers had come out of Germany and that that was going to change the nature of our discussion with the Europeans.

After I took my new job, my bosses told me the White House was extremely interested in Iraq and that we should report everything we could find out about it, as well as on Iran and China. The scuttlebutt in the agency back then was that the Bush people were out to settle the score for the Gulf War, which ended with Saddam still in place. At the time, I too thought they saw Iraq as unfinished business. But it was less Freudian and more banal than that. After Yasser Arafat walked away from the peace deal at the end of the Clinton administration, they truly believed there was no solution to the Israeli–Palestinian conflict along that route and that if they could just knock out the dictatorship in Iraq and put in a favorable government, Iraq would become a bastion of democracy and a base for the United States in the Middle East. This view, most strongly held by the hawks in the administration—the likes of Donald Rumsfeld, the secretary of defense, and his deputy Paul Wolfowitz, who has become synonymous with the Iraq War—seemed to find a willing ear in the

president, perhaps especially since Saddam had tried to assassinate his father. At the time, I didn't see where this coincidence of
interests was going to lead us.

In the meantime, I had several sessions with Cofer Black, who
was extremely frustrated about what he saw as a lack of traction
on counterterrorist issues among the Europeans. We resolved to
visit Europe in October to try to speak to our allies about what
he saw as the biggest problem—their laws protecting people's
right to privacy, which are tougher than ours and which he said
would have to be changed to accommodate the need to detain
suspects. One of his big concerns was that potential terrorists
would hide behind European asylum laws, for example. My position was that we should work with our friends instead of tackling
them head-on on such a politically sensitive issue. There was a
risk, I argued, that they would simply dig in their heels and get
angry at an attempt to meddle in their domestic concerns. With
one European ally in particular, we also had to deal with the
impact of a misunderstanding between us that led each side to
suspect the other of intransigence and unwillingness to share
intelligence. I am happy to say this misunderstanding has since
been largely cleared up. But at the time, we wanted human intelligence from them and instead got analysis, and they wanted
analysis from us and instead got human intelligence. I said to
Tenet shortly before he met the head of that country's service
after 9/11 that we would be best served by an accommodating
approach rather than a confrontational one, and he took my
advice. But the thrust of the Bush administration's approach has
been to continue to persuade the Europeans in general to water
down their privacy laws, an approach that has only made it
harder to work with our counterparts there.

"Rather than complain about the Europeans all the time, let's try to make use of what they have," I said to Cofer. "So you sit down and talk to them and I'll be there to stop you guys from strangling each other. We all know you think they're feckless but that doesn't do us any good, so let's try to work with them."

"All right, all right," he said. "Let's do it."

But the momentum for that visit, as, no doubt, with countless other small initiatives, died when we went into crisis mode after 9/11. I don't believe we've come to the surface since.

At that time, Tenet was also focused on cooperating with the Europeans while understanding their sensitivities. He and I did discuss making a dramatic change in the way we worked with the Europeans so that we could break down the traditional intelligence barriers that existed between us on terrorist issues. Tenet really believed in this principle, but he wasn't strong enough to make it happen. It could have led to a profoundly different way of approaching intelligence with the European services and it was beginning to show success before I left, though not as extensively as I would have liked. The idea met with tremendous resistance from the Counterterrorist Center, which was worried that our cooperation would backfire because of relations between Europeans and Middle Eastern countries, and from other elements of the agency, including the Bin Laden unit. It went against our entire culture. The conventional wisdom was that we would be giving away all our secrets. That kind of thinking drove Tenet crazy. Nothing would make him angrier—in fact it would make him explode—than when someone would ask in a meeting, "Have you told the Europeans?" and the answer would come back, "Well, now, that comes from a very sensitive source . . ."

I admired this determination to break down barriers with our allies, but he was swimming against the tide, which was turning increasingly away from the real targets and toward Iraq.

The Bush administration was about to embark on a course that would do more to undermine this country's intelligence community than any of the actions of its predecessors.

Chapter Two†

DOWN THE RABBIT HOLE

Langley, Virginia. September 12, 2001

A mid all the emotion following that terrible day, there was a moment of clarity when everyone believed we would focus on overthrowing the Taliban and capturing Osama bin Laden. Our closest allies believed it, too, at first, and with some justification.

I will never forget the day after 9/11, when the first flight allowed into U.S. airspace brought in a powerful delegation from a very close European ally, led by an able diplomat who has been rewarded for his work during this period, and the head of

† **Publisher's note:** The nationality of the visiting delegation in this chapter and other details of what the author witnessed of that event have been masked under CIA secrecy requirements.

29

its foreign service, who won respect on this side of the Atlantic for serving his country so ably. The sky over Washington was eerily empty of the passenger jets that normally swoop low over the skyscrapers of northern Virginia and along the Potomac River into Reagan National Airport. Only the distant rumble of patrolling fighter jets was to be heard. For some, it was comforting, as it meant someone was watching over us. For others, it was unnerving, a constant reminder—and some might say an unnecessary one—that we were at war.

Andrews Air Force Base, a sprawling, anonymous place to the southeast of downtown Washington, D.C., has launched many a diplomatic mission by the United States. This time the diplomats were coming to us, the wounded party, bearing advice and seeking reassurances. Overnight, Andrews had changed dramatically. It went from a rather quiet military installation where dignitaries were politely asked to show their ID to a scene from a war movie, with heavily armed soldier after heavily armed soldier guarding the roadways and every vehicle checked thoroughly.

A fleet of limousines swept our visitors across town to the Virginia suburbs, where they were to dine with the heads of covert and overt law enforcement in the reception rooms at the CIA. We were too many to fit into Tenet's personal dining room, so we used another executive room, a rather soulless place with blue walls and tables covered in crisp white linen and arranged in a square. There was an air of surrealism about the whole late-night gathering, as white-jacketed waiters moved quietly around the tables and served us food.

The goal was to agree on a war plan and decide what to do in Europe to defeat the terrorists. The attendees included Cofer

Black, Jim Pavitt, Associate Deputy Director of Operations Hugh Turner, the acting director of the FBI Thomas Pickard, CIA Executive Director Buzzy Krongard, the chief of the Near East division, and me.

The head of the visiting delegation opened our discussion in the seventh-floor dining room of headquarters with a heartfelt statement of support for the United States.

For a dry guy, he was quite emotional. He wanted us to know that his government stood by us in our time of need and that we could count on it for any and all support. After the pleasantries came the kicker. The delegation leader ended his remarks by saying he hoped there was no desire to include Iraq in any actions. "I hope we can all agree that we should concentrate on Afghanistan and not be tempted to launch any attacks on Iraq."

"Absolutely, we all agree on that," Tenet said. "Some might want to link the issues, but none of us wants to go that route," he added. Everyone at the CIA was of the opinion that we should concentrate on Afghanistan and avoid the temptation of Iraq. No one needed to be reminded of who was on the other side of this argument—Wolfowitz, Rumsfeld, Vice President Dick Cheney, and the others—but for now the intelligence community on both sides of the Atlantic was on the same page.

The good-feeling bubble burst quickly, however. Right on cue, Pavitt's chief of staff walked in with a cable. Tenet and his boss would not like it, he warned. Pavitt read it and agreed with the assessment. He passed it to Tenet, who was less than thrilled! "I thought nothing like this was supposed to go out without our OK." Pavitt, looking rather sheepish, said he would take care of it.

After dinner, as everyone split up into smaller groups, the chief of staff revealed the contents of the cable to me. It was addressed to CIA paramilitaries in Afghanistan, written by a branch of the Counterterrorist Center, and approved by one of Cofer's deputies. If Bin Laden were killed, it said, they should send us some physical evidence, preferably body parts, or language to that effect. I was at a loss for words. We were supposed to be too professional and focused to indulge in that kind of talk. Looking back, I see this as the first appearance of the heated rhetoric that did nothing to help our cause, a symptom of the thinking fostered by an administration that did not set out a clear policy in response to the attacks.

I don't know what our European visitors thought about all this. Perhaps they were just too polite to say. Tenet's visiting counterpart was a spy's spy and usually incredibly hard to read. It's hard even to describe him physically—a mark of an excellent undercover agent. He is more or less of average height with a hawkish nose—or maybe not. I saw him work the American intelligence community brilliantly. Whereas our senior leaders are often drawn from political ranks, he had been an extremely successful case officer. He thought operationally, was very good at making contacts and extracting the maximum benefit from them, and enjoyed a close relationship with Tenet, leading his country to gain unprecedented access to our intelligence on terrorist matters and the closest cooperation since World War II.

I would argue that we must foster exactly this type of closeness between allies if we are to make any real progress in waging war against terrorism. The CIA has always strived to manage its relationship with this crucial ally extremely carefully, and I believe this administration has hurt this effort. From the 1980s until Tenet came into office, CIA management kept the relationship under tight control. It was the height of the Cold War, and our counterparts were just as aggressive as we were in their pursuit of targets. As a result, we found ourselves bumping into each other all the time, for example in Africa, where there was a limited number of individuals to go after and we sometimes became mired in counterproductive squabbling at lower levels. Eventually Tenet straightened this out by insisting that such turf battles be settled at a senior level. I often found myself having to manage such collisions of interest in my role as European division chief, which led to fewer problems on the ground.

Tenet also committed himself to taking advantage of the excellent work our closest European allies can do, developing very close personal relationships with his counterparts. In the run-up to the 2000 presidential election, when President Bush first took office, this particular ally's leadership was extremely concerned that Tenet might leave and be replaced by a more cautious individual, and that Pavitt would leave. They were relieved to find that both stayed put, though the respite was to be temporary.

Many at the CIA remain wary of the closeness of this relationship, and I am sorry to say that I have not detected any strong direction in this regard from Porter Goss. But as long as we remember that our foreign counterparts serve their government first, they remain an invaluable asset.

That night, as we tried to absorb the reality of the bloodshed of the day before, I sat down with one of the senior allied representatives. We agreed to try to make the pursuit of Al Qaeda seem like a multinational effort, to include the other Europeans as much as possible. I knew some of our European friends would work more easily with this country than they would with us, a natural consequence of their participation in the European Union. I thought European governments might take a demand for closer cooperation on terrorism better from one of their neighbors than they would from us.

That is why it frustrates the hell out of me that this administration has damaged our relations with European countries over the past few years. When Rumsfeld, in January 2003, dismissed France and Germany, two of our most useful allies, as "Old Europe," it perfectly expressed the administration's wrongheaded perspective. Had I known what was to come, I would have done more to make them understand the value of our friends across the ocean. Then again, with their agendas, their minds were already made up.

We left the meeting with a pledge of commitment to work with us against the terrorists who had struck on American soil but, as has since tragically been proven, could equally take aim elsewhere, for example in Madrid and London. Everyone was determined to put our resources into the effort to oust the Taliban and hunt down Bin Laden in Afghanistan. The visit left us all with the strong impression that this closest of allies would stand with us and help facilitate our relationships with other European countries. But we understood just as clearly that our ally wanted us to heed its advice not to unleash a war in Iraq. We at the agency believed, wrongly as it turned out, that the Bush administration would in the end avoid going down that path.

Four days later, I attended a follow-up discussion with our foreign friends, this time on their turf, a rather charmless building on Washington's otherwise more picturesque embassy row.

It was 5 P.M., mercifully near the end of one of those intense, sweltering days that sometimes hit Washington in early fall, as we pulled up at the gates. We were all dressed casually, it being a Sunday, apart from Cofer, a very dedicated fellow, who, like

Tenet, took the 9/11 attacks incredibly hard—like a personal failure. He hadn't left his post since the day the planes hit the World Trade Center—in fact, five days later, Pavitt would order him home—so he turned up that day in the same suit he had worn for days, quite literally wearing his anger on his sleeve. He has a self-deprecating sense of humor and is a genuinely nice guy in happier times, an excellent speaker with a straight way of talking. But he's also emotional, and on that day, he was uncharacteristically blunt, to the point of being unfriendly. The head of the CIA's paramilitary division, euphemistically called "Special Activities," and the deputy chief of the Near East division joined us for a meeting that came in response to a request from our allies, who had let us know that they were still worried about what we were going to do next.

The rest of the world was waiting nervously to see what we would do in Afghanistan. As the head of the European division, it was my job to keep our allies engaged in planning.

We briefed our colleagues, who included two senior counterterrorism officials from the allied country and their local representative, about how we planned to crush the Taliban and kill Osama bin Laden and his followers in Afghanistan. It was strange for us to be talking like that. But they were strange times.

Cofer presented a new presidential authorization that broadened our options for dealing with terrorist targets—one of the few times such a thing had happened since the CIA was officially banned from carrying out assassinations in 1976. It was clear that the administration saw this as a war that would largely be fought by intelligence assets. This required a new way of operating. The management of the clandestine service recognized the need for new tactics, but we also knew the complications involved in managing these operations. The need for this attention to detail was another reason for our concern about potential distractions in Iraq. Our allies mulled over the proposals. They clearly had concerns.

What are you going to do, asked the visiting top counterterrorist official, once you've "hit the mercury with the hammer in Afghanistan and the Al Qaeda cadre has spread all over the Middle East?"

"Aren't you concerned," he asked in a measured voice, "about the potential destabilizing effect on Middle Eastern countries?"

"No," Cofer said. "Our only concern is killing terrorists." One of my European colleagues and I, understanding Cofer's state of mind, did our best to contain the damage. Cofer was tired, my foreign friend said, conveying the message that we had not collectively gone mad, that we were just responding to the horror of the attacks. I quickly told our counterparts that, in fact, we were indeed concerned about avoiding any unintended consequences from our actions in Afghanistan or elsewhere in the war on terrorism, though it wasn't that cut and dried. "Well, you can do what you want," Cofer said, looking on gloomily.

After three hours of discussions in this vein, we left the meeting. The counterterrorist official said, as we walked along the corridor: "All rather bloodcurdling, isn't it?" I didn't quite know what to say.

On the surface, our visitors seemed laid-back. But it was clear they were worried, and not without reason. We weren't thinking straight, and the Bush administration was already headed in the wrong direction. Rumsfeld started trying to link Iraq to Al Qaeda almost as soon as the attacks happened, as CBS News would later report. Within fifteen minutes of the attacks, the National Security

Agency intercepted a call from an Al Qaeda operative in Asia to a contact in a former Soviet republic reporting the "good news" of the attacks in New York and on the Pentagon. Tenet passed that report on to Rumsfeld around midday, but according to notes taken by aides who were with the secretary of defense, he characterized the NSA report as "vague" and said there was "no good basis for hanging hat" on the fact that Al Qaeda had conducted the assaults. Later that afternoon, CIA intelligence showing that three of the hijackers were suspected Al Qaeda men was still not enough for Rumsfeld. As he ordered his military to start work on retaliatory strikes, he said he wanted "best info fast," and issued instructions to "[j]udge whether good enough hit S. H. at same time. Not only UBL," referring respectively to Saddam Hussein and Osama bin Laden. The seeds were already being sown for a war built on a house of cards that in my opinion would distract us from the real targets in the war on terrorism.

Right after the meeting, Cofer said to me that we would probably all end up getting indicted for some of the things we would have to do to win the war. He was speaking cryptically, hinting at the theoretical consequences of the more unsavory actions we might have to take to catch the terrorists, though with his presentation, he almost appeared to be relishing the prospect. Many of us were being ruled by our hearts at a time when we desperately needed clear direction from our heads, and more importantly, our leaders. We all knew we were facing a long, probably dirty war and that some people on our side might want to exact revenge, and we were going to have to be thoughtful about how we approached the coming confrontations.

--

The chief concern of our allies was that we would start taking unilateral actions on European turf, notably by plucking suspected terrorists off their soil without their permission and sending them to a third country. They worried, with some justification, that such "renditions" would create political difficulties for them at home. They expressed this concern to me personally, and to the chiefs of stations in their capitals. You need to understand, we told them, that we have been attacked, and our attackers didn't fly here from Kabul. In many cases, they came via Europe, and we need to be able to stop them in the future.

On the face of it, this should have been an easy argument to win. Four of the 9/11 plotters had formed a cell in Hamburg before coming to the United States. One was Mohammed Atta, who flew American Airlines Flight 11 into the north tower of the World Trade Center. Another was Marwan al-Shehhi, who slammed United Airlines Flight 175 into the south tower sixteen minutes and thirty-one seconds later.

So we worked on securing agreements from foreign governments that we would all redouble our efforts to catch militants. It was the best defense against being attacked again, and against the kind of "bloodcurdling" unilateral actions at which my colleague had hinted. We promised to include our allies in operations, but we could not make any promises about unilateral actions. We were keeping our options open, particularly since we were operating in a policy vacuum.

The very morning of our meeting at the embassy, Cheney had made that clear, telling NBC's *Meet the Press* program:

> We also have to work, though, sort of the dark side, if
> you will. We've got to spend time in the shadows in

the intelligence world. A lot of what needs to be done here will have to be done quietly, without any discussion, using sources and methods that are available to our intelligence agencies, if we're going to be successful. That's the world these folks operate in, and so it's going to be vital for us to use any means at our disposal, basically, to achieve our objective.

He was waving a huge red flag when it would have been better to say nothing, to allow us to do our jobs quietly, to promise the American people that their government would do everything it could to protect them by pursuing the terrorists and leave it at that. Every responsible chief in the CIA knows that the more covert the action, the greater the need for a clear policy and a defined target. When Cheney spoke those words, he was articulating a policy that amounted to "go out and get 'em." His remarks were evidence of the underlying approach of the administration, which was basically to turn the military and agency loose and let them pay for the consequences of any unfortunate—or illegal—occurrences. By saying such things in public and in such an emotional way, he also made our jobs harder by alarming our allies in Europe. The remarks served no useful international purpose. I can only assume they were intended for domestic consumption. But they were unhelpful, to say the least.

From the perspective of the White House, it was smart to blur the lines about what was acceptable and what was not in the war on terrorism. It meant that whenever someone was overzealous in some dark interrogation cell at an undisclosed location, or whenever an immature, inadequately trained soldier stripped, humiliated, or beat a detainee in Iraq, President Bush and his entourage could blame someone else. And in fact, despite all the investigations and commissions and panels that have examined the intelligence failures and prisoner abuses since September 11, not once have the politicians truly been taken to task. To paraphrase Truman, with the Bush administration, the buck stops anywhere but on their desks.

It is in this light that I believe the media reports of maltreatment of prisoners in Iraq should be read. If people are to be blamed for any mishandling of detainees, I believe in general that any individual officers on the scene should not be turned into scapegoats, because that way the problems will never be fixed. Only by undertaking an honest evaluation of any errors made throughout the chain of command, from top to bottom, can we ensure this never happens again. Any problems that arose were surely related to unclear orders they were given, or guidelines they were not given. Overall, the greater responsibility devolves not just to theater commanders, but rather to the policy itself, which propagates the treatment of such detainees as men who are guilty before trial, who are terrorists and criminals rather than prisoners of war deserving protections under the Geneva conventions. Such overgeneralization is exactly the kind of thing that can lead to abuses. People need clear rules. That is how our society is set up. That is how we make it easier for our courts to identify wrongdoers. Regardless of the nature of dramatic, overheated rhetoric early in a struggle, in the end the American people always want the rule of law to prevail. This is what makes us a great country. The people in Iraq, on all sides of the matter, military and civilian, American, Sunni, Shiite, and Christian, deserve no less.

After September 11, our government sent people out, all fired up, to catch or kill terrorists who to them were the living embod-iment of the hijackers. They thought they were carrying out the policy and the will of the American people, and, more impor-tantly, of the president.

Perhaps that is why my colorful colleague, Cofer Black, used to talk so much about how we had to "put flies on their eyeballs" to win the war.

Even as there was a lack of direction on the ground in Iraq, Cheney and, to a lesser extent, Bush, made their presence felt at the CIA far more frequently than any previous administration I am aware of. In the case of Cheney, this trend sometimes mani-fested itself in unusual ways. One incident in particular sticks out in my mind.

My office filed a report containing a comment from a Euro-pean leader about Cheney that was not remotely insulting. I dis-seminated it to the White House, as was protocol, in order to reduce the risk it would leak out and create unwelcome head-lines, and it should have gone straight to him. The next thing I know I'm in Pavitt's office, getting yelled at. What happened was that Condoleezza Rice, who was national security adviser at the time, had asked Cheney if he'd seen it, and he hadn't. A senior member of his staff called up Pavitt, livid, demanding to know how we dared put out a report referring to the vice president without notifying them, accusing us of trying to embarrass Cheney and asking what our agenda was. We had in fact followed the usual procedure, which was to limit the distribution list to the top of the administration, including Cheney. It wasn't my fault he didn't read it. They implied, however, that I was trying to embarrass the vice president. I wasn't. I was just doing my job.

This event clearly demonstrated how nervous the administration was making everyone. For something so minor, one of my oldest colleagues, someone with whom I shared a mutual admiration and friendship, had chewed me up as badly as I'd ever been chewed up in my career. After Pavitt settled down, he said he was under a lot of stress and pressure from Cheney's office and apologized—he knew we hadn't done anything wrong.

I think now that Cheney and others in the administration see everything through such a political prism that it never crossed the minds of his staff members that I might have been innocently doing my job, just as I always had. They had to examine my actions for any hint of a political motive, to see if there were any political consequences to be calculated.

In the past, this would never have happened. I remember that, when Bill Clinton became president, we were hearing that European leaders were concerned he lacked sophistication as a former governor from Arkansas and were worried about his emphasis on domestic concerns, which won him the election from the first President Bush, with his more international flavor. The Europeans were speculating that they would have to work through Vice President Al Gore as the one with greater understanding of foreign policy, particularly with the problems in Yugoslavia, which had broken apart and erupted in war while Bush senior was in office.

But when this reporting went back to Washington, we never heard anything about Clinton being upset that disparaging remarks were being made, or faced criticism for passing this information on. We received the appropriate response, which was to weigh the implications of these European concerns. And Clinton wore down the Europeans until they eventually embraced him.

After the incident with Cheney, any time we got any reporting in my division that referred to him, however obliquely, we made doubly sure that someone at the National Security Council was specifically notified and instructed to alert Cheney to the document, however good, bad, or indifferent it might be.

The other way Cheney made his presence felt was by visiting Langley regularly, perhaps six or seven times that I can recall, including two or three times after the Iraq War had begun, when the search for weapons of mass destruction in Iraq was going so badly. Though I did not attend his meetings, close colleagues would talk about preparations for them. The general feeling was that they amounted to a distraction that ate up a whole day in preparations, and an inappropriate involvement of the executive branch at a level of operational detail that was uncomfortable. In my opinion, his repeated visits had the effect of underscoring his unblinking conviction and unshakeable commitment to the idea that Iraq was an immediate threat. They were a manifestation of the emphasis on using the agency to justify the war. I have to assume he was no less emphatic in his convictions about Saddam's capabilities in private than he was in public.

A close colleague of mine also told me that a special reading room had been set up for him to survey classified documents. While it was not unprecedented for a vice president to visit the agency, none of my colleagues can remember a vice president visiting as often as Cheney did. The agency should be independent of political influence, operating on professionalism and fact. This often upsets powerful people in the government, but history has shown that it is crucial to having a professional intelligence service carrying out espionage in the world without the crippling effects of political bias. Increasingly in the aftermath of 9/11, it felt as if we had been subsumed into the world of the White House. The only way to get ahead, it was sensed by everyone, was not only to catch suspects, but also to go along with the master plan for the Middle East.

In the midst of all that, ethical questions became blurred. I once had to brief Rice on a rendition operation, and her chief concern was not whether it was the right thing to do, but what the president would think about it. I would have expected a big meeting, a debate about whether to proceed with the plan, a couple of hours' consideration of the pros and cons. We should have been talking about the value of the target, whether the threat he presented warranted such a potentially controversial intervention, what the impact on our relations abroad would be. Instead, we got no direction, just an approving response and a "We'll have to figure out how to tell the president." This is no way to run a covert policy. If the White House wants to take extraordinary measures to win the war on terrorism, it has to be willing to face its responsibility for approving sensitive operations without meddling in the actual work of carrying them out, and not just approve them without getting into a discussion about their value and morality, like a bureaucrat who can later say, well, it wasn't my fault, I was only the rubber stamp and I didn't have all the information about what was going to happen.

President Bush did take a direct interest in intelligence operations, when it suited him. I am reminded of a day I went to see John McLaughlin, Tenet's deputy, about sharing information with the ally that was publicly our most vocal critic where it came to Iraq, on an important and worrisome operation for which they had reporting that would improve our understanding of the matter. I wanted to pursue the matter with them, but suddenly I found myself facing a new challenge to my work. "We will have to ask the president," McLaughlin said. "The president of the United States?" I asked. John nodded. "The president is the case officer on this one."

To this day the United States still does not have a clear policy on renditions and repatriations of detainees, especially if they are being returned to countries where they might be tortured. I have very complicated feelings about the whole issue. I would be lying if I said I had no involvement in renditions. I know that we would be insane to leave someone free to carry out an attack. But torture is obviously wrong and, operationally speaking, it doesn't work. You can't trust intelligence that comes from someone who has been brought to within an inch of his life, and you certainly can't take it to trial.

I was disappointed to read media reports, for example in the *New York Times* in May 2004, saying that American interrogators had used extreme measures against Khalid Sheikh Mohammed, the 9/11 mastermind who was captured in Pakistan. It has also been reported that we refused to hand him over for questioning in the case of Zacarias Moussaoui, the alleged twentieth hijacker, whose trial dragged on interminably and eventually ended with him pleading guilty but denying he was part of the September 11 plot. Such are the complications that can arise when a witness has undergone extreme interrogation tactics.

I was also taken aback to read in published reports of the deaths of suspects in U.S. custody in Afghanistan. If these reports are true—and I honestly do not know if they are—as a human being, it goes against the grain for me to defend these policies. But as a CIA officer, my concerns would be: does it work, and does it distract us from the real business of finding sources who will warn us of future attacks? The answers are clearly no, and yes.

Having said that, I do see the purpose of renditions, if they are carried out properly. Guys sitting around talking about carrying out attacks as they smoke their pipes in the comfort of a European capital tend to get put off the idea if they learn that a like-minded individual has been plucked out of safety and sent elsewhere to pay for his crimes. To the outside world, it might look like a vengeful act, as if an innocent had been sent to a country with a record of torture, for example in one of a number of countries in the Middle East. People always suspect the CIA of doing bad things because they can. I'm sure there are people like in that in my profession, but in my experience they are not the ones who win respect and favor. A cool head and a moral compass are both essentials of my craft.

It is worth mentioning that it is typical that an allied government will have information on potential terrorists that has been collected through intelligence channels and cannot be used in court. In those narrow instances, rendition is clearly called for, since there is no other option, until we and our allies have developed an alternative strategy to operating in the shadows, and until the public has had a chance to approve guidelines. When Bush won his second election, he clearly felt he had been given permission to continue to avoid his responsibility for renditions and other, more unsavory elements of the war on terrorism, and I fear for the long-term consequences.

One case that I believe could act as a template for renditions unfolded in a European capital in the fall of 1998. Local law-enforcement officers there questioned and eventually expelled a Sudanese suspect that year, disrupting the planning of attacks against the U.S. embassy. We would have liked to hold the fellow ourselves, but there were no warrants on him in the United States. So we settled for having him expelled to Sudan and alerting other European countries to the potential danger. He later tried to return to another European country, but was denied entry.

In the end, the operation worked because the Europeans had good information developed from their own sources, and we were well supported by the FBI and the CIA unit that was tracking Bin Laden. Obviously, the biggest problem here is the value of the information, so we need strong oversight of the trustworthiness of the source. The Curveball case, which we'll get to later, is a case in point.

Another controversial case I have read about involved a pair of renditions, also in Europe. The suspects, from a Middle Eastern country, were seeking political asylum. The European country in question contacted us and said they were worried the two men were planning an attack that would affect American interests and they wanted them out of their jurisdiction. Their homeland was all too happy to have them returned to serve jail sentences for alleged terrorist activities.

The European country's foreign minister decided to expel the men, and the ruling was swiftly carried out. Agents from the local security police picked them up off the streets of the capital. They were driven to a nearby airport where, according to a Swedish documentary broadcast on TV4's *Kalla Fakta* program, a group of men alighted from a U.S.-leased jet, took them to a small room with their hands and feet chained, cut their clothes from their bodies, inserted suppositories in their rectums (apparently to administer a tranquilizer), and dressed them in diapers and dark overalls. The plane flew them to a Middle Eastern capital as agreed, the documentary claimed.

The men have since alleged they were tortured in their homeland. I have no way of knowing if this is true, but obviously I would rather it were not. The point is that the Europeans thought the men were going to carry out a terrorist attack and they were legally repatriated to the country of their birth to face criminal charges. If the rendition team had avoided the unnecessary excesses and treated the detainees properly, as the specific situation indicated, this could have been a good example of a rendition working well. Instead, the case illustrates how much thought has to go into such an operation. Most cases I have seen have been handled carefully, but there is always room for controversy to develop. The whole process calls for serious oversight. For me, the reports of the hoods and the suppositories and the unnecessary maltreatment are symptoms of the worst kind of bureaucratic groupthink. They are a twenty-first-century, post–September 11 example of the "banality of evil" lamented by Hannah Arendt. She coined the memorable phrase to remind us that evil can seem harmless and ordinary when twisted policy rules a bureaucracy.

The rendition teams are drawn from paramilitary officers, who are brave and colorful. They are the men who went into Baghdad before the bombs and into Afghanistan before the army. If they didn't do paramilitary actions for a living, they'd probably be robbing banks. So any politician who pretends to be surprised at the consequences when they set these guys loose without clear policy direction is either kidding himself or lying. These men know that the fellow they are dealing with is a terrorist suspect and he might be wearing a bomb, or he might have AIDS and bite him, so they, not surprisingly, believe extraordinary measures are justified. They are not nuts. If you're getting on a plane with someone and all you know about them is that they are a terrorist suspect, you too would want to be sure they were not going to blow you up. It would be naive to expect these men to stop and think about the diplomatic consequences when they cut their captives' clothes off in the middle of a swanky European capital. And I'm sure that for some of these men, there is a lust for vengeance. So the rules must be clear and strictly enforced.

Some of my old colleagues will point out that these teams have detailed operational instructions. But it is clear policy from the top that really sets the parameters for these types of operations. Bush or Cheney saying that we are going to hunt down the terrorists and "get them" leaves these brave officers out on a limb, believing they are carrying out the spirit of what their leaders want, only to be called to question when their operations become public and people are disturbed. This is especially true when these revelations cause political problems. These officers and the dedicated counterterrorist officers who direct them deserve better. More than that, the whole question of the rendition program is a reflection of the confusion over the responsibilities in the war on terrorism. The White House never established a long-term solution for the men who have ended up in Guantanamo Bay or the other undisclosed locations where suspects are held, and never defined the target clearly, so the United States has just kept driving forward with renditions. We never defined our target. Bush has drawn the war in the simplest of terms, saying it is being fought to preserve our "way of life," but that is not a policy, and I'm not even sure it's accurate. A lot of the men who fought for Bin Laden know barely anything about our way of life, and I suspect that if they did, they wouldn't be fighting to end it. In fact, they would probably be fighting to join it. Perhaps the Bush administration deliberately created a gray area on renditions—that would be in keeping with a White House that seems so tightly managed in almost every other respect. Whatever this unclear policy's purpose, instead of turning on the services involved when things don't go right, the leadership should be creating clear lines for the case officers in the field, not serving them up with platitudes.

The *Washington Post*'s Dana Priest ran a story on December 4, 2005, that is an excellent example of how things can go wrong; and when there are mistakes, they must be quickly rectified. According to this article, authorities focused on Khaled al-Masri, a German citizen whose name matched that of a man believed to have trained in an Al Qaeda camp. He was seized in Macedonia on New Year's Eve 2003 after local authorities said his passport was fake, and, three weeks later, sent to a detention center in Afghanistan, the report stated. By March, Langley discovered that his passport was genuine, and that they had the wrong fellow in custody, the report said. But it took until late May for him to be released, after a debate between the State Department and the CIA over how much to tell the Germans about what had happened.

It is essential that we get the targeting of suspects right. The terrorists hide out in urban communities around the world, recruiting from among disaffected men—and occasionally women—who sympathize with them. This is what the CIA does best, recruit and handle agents. There is no reason why the skills the agency acquired in the Cold War cannot be turned to good effect by being used to penetrate émigré communities to find helpful sources. Then we can work with the local authorities to monitor closely the dangerous smaller groups, using the appropriate authorities to act if they appear to be going into an operational stance. Iraq has made this effort harder. At first, there really was no link between the war and the fight against international terrorism, except perhaps to demonstrate the power of the U.S. military to the terrorists, or governments that deal with them. But the war has turned Iraq into a magnet and training ground for new terrorists who want to strike at the United States. At the same time, because we are having so much difficulty subduing the insurgents and foreign fighters in Iraq, other potential terrorists are losing the fear of the U.S. military that they felt after the attack on Afghanistan. This is dangerous on two fronts. First, it emboldens terrorists, and second, it results in them not realizing that what is going on in Iraq does not represent the full power of the U.S. military—which would be unleashed if there is another attack on American soil.

The only way we will ever be able to protect ourselves properly is if we can get a handle on the threat in Europe, since that is the continent where fanatics can best learn their most crucial lesson—how to disappear in a Western crowd. This was an issue of concern even before I retired, a trend we were hearing about from European services. Europe has become a training ground for terrorists, especially since the war in Iraq has heralded an underground railroad for militants to go and fight in Iraq. They cited evidence that a well-established route for illegal immigrants from the Middle East to Europe worked both ways. It is being used for young fanatics in Europe to be smuggled into Iraq to fight Americans and, assuming they survive, to return home, where they present a more potent threat than they did before they left.

Since the odds against penetrating the top of Al Qaeda are

phenomenally high, we must pursue these foot soldiers. The value in befriending the local intelligence services in Europe instead of alienating them is clear; we need to ensure they are telling us everything they know. I often wonder whether, the next time police in the European country where the two Middle Eastern suspects were seized spot some suspects in their midst, they will think long and hard before getting the United States involved. It certainly won't help our arguments to pursue terrorist threats in Europe if the United States mishandles renditions. I personally experienced a number of situations where we had a concern that a particular institution or mosque was being used to foment terrorism and a host nation disagreed about the value of following up, hampering our intelligence-gathering efforts.

A good example of international cooperation was the case of the alleged leader of Ansar Al-Islam, the Iraqi-based group linked to Al Qaeda, who was living in Europe. We helped the European court by bringing prosecutors and defense attorneys to Iraq to interview captured fighters who said he had sent them there to carry out suicide bombings. The minute the defense teams started to interview them, the suspects said they had been tortured—which they hadn't been, to the best of my knowledge.

The case is still tied up in court, and some might say the militant leader is still a threat because he is not behind bars. At the time of writing, a European court had ruled that he should be expelled to Iraq once the situation there stabilized. The point is that whatever his guilt or otherwise, he was effectively neutralized. He could not go anywhere without people knowing about it. So our job was done. Needless to say, the alternative espoused by midlevel people at the Pentagon was to send out a team of Navy SEALs—the guys you see in the movies rolling up in the dead of night on a foreign shore—to grab the suspect if the Europeans wouldn't cooperate. But we took our time and worked with the European justice system, accomplishing our goal while improving our relations with the European country in question.

——

In October, I found myself again having to reassure my British colleagues that we were not going to attack Iraq. I traveled with Tenet to London to attend a memorial for David Spedding, the head of the foreign service from 1994 to 1999, who died in June at the age of fifty-eight from lung cancer. On the sidelines of the memorial, the hope was expressed that "we all agree that Iraq is not on, that we have no evidence of a link." I passed this piece of reporting on to my superiors through the usual channels. "We should focus on Afghanistan," one of Spedding's colleagues said, and I agreed. "If you go into Iraq," he said, "it's really going to complicate things." I told him there were people in the administration who wanted to do just that, but that Tenet and Powell, as was widely reported at the time, were dead against it. I heard Tenet say numerous times until some weeks before the war began that there was no link to Iraq and we had to focus on terrorism, and I was confident, as I told my counterpart, that Tenet had the president's ear.

Despite the concerns about a premature attack on Saddam Hussein, European services offered excellent cooperation through the end of the year. The swiftness with which the Taliban fell, in November, seemed to be having a positive effect on intelligence gathering in the Middle East, too: there was a widespread feeling of good will toward the United States and a sense that we had a right to defend ourselves. The effectiveness of the attacks surprised European governments, who had expected us to get bogged down in a Soviet-style quagmire.

It's good for your enemies to think you're a little crazy, a British colleague said. As long as you can back it up. Those words would ring in my ears later, as we got sucked down the rabbit hole into Iraq.

Chapter Three

OVERLOOKED ALLIES

Ankara, Turkey. April 2002

As I look back on the spring and fall of 2002, I believe problems in the administration's war planning were multiplied by policy miscalculations toward key allies like Turkey. This sad story is well documented in the press; how U.S. war planners misread dramatically the changes that had occurred in Turkish politics. Their planning made assumptions that kept the Fourth Infantry Division of the U.S. Army out of the initial fighting in Iraq, and perhaps more importantly, out of the early stages of the occupation. The presence of these highly trained, well-equipped troops would have helped limit the looting and property destruction that followed the fall of

Baghdad, which laid the groundwork for the ongoing insurgency. In 1990 the then secular government of Turkey had supported the allies in Desert Storm, but by 2002 the government in Ankara was in the hands of the moderate Islamist Refah Party, and in the opinion of many observers was unlikely to become deeply involved in any U.S. attack on northern Iraq.

But Turkey was not the only ally whose views, in my opinion, were overlooked.

Even Britain, our closest ally, would have preferred if we had waited longer before invading. Downing Street repeatedly sought reassurances after the September 11 attacks that we would not widen the scope of the war. I believe that the Bush administration also did unnecessary damage to our relations with France, a country that is a natural ally in the war against terrorism, having suffered similar terrorist threats.

I was shocked when Rumsfeld, in television interviews in March 2005, failed to take any responsibility for the failure of the Turkish gamble, as he faulted this crucial NATO ally instead of acknowledging the truth: that its circumstances had changed dramatically since the Gulf War and that public opinion would not have tolerated the use of Turkish soil to invade its neighbor. Rumsfeld brazenly said the insurgency would have been smaller had Turkey given its permission, implying that the Turks had cost American lives. It is equally true that had we been more sensitive to Turkish domestic concerns, we would have understood that we could not count on Turkey and made different—and smarter—preparations for the invasion. As Wolfowitz made painfully clear when he gleefully told reporters during a visit to Ankara that "Turkish support is assured,"* the ideologues at the Pentagon and the war planners must have been thinking that they could force the country to go along. To my mind, this was one of the failings of the war cry proclaimed so bluntly by President Bush nine days after September 11 in an address before Congress: "Either you are with us, or you are with the terrorists." It was obvious to everyone that many countries would have to juggle domestic and foreign interests in their stance in the war on terrorism, and Turkey was no exception. The Turks really were caught in the middle. Recep Tayyip Erdogan, who had previously been banned from running for office because of his pro-Islamist views but would eventually become prime minister, wanted to help despite his Islamist roots and had no love for Saddam Hussein. But we had staked out no middle ground for Turkey to occupy and we ended up with nothing. Just as the administration gambled on finding weapons in Iraq while ignoring our evidence to the contrary, in my opinion it ignored the obvious fact that the Turks felt too pinched by political crisis to take another risk on an American intervention on their doorstep.

An additional complication, in my opinion, was the conflict between the military's Central Command, which has responsibility for countries stretching from the horn of Africa to central Asia, and its European Command, which covers Europe, the rest of Africa, and the Middle East. The latter was sensitive to Turkish concerns, having worked with the country for years. Central Command, meanwhile, ignored the looming complication and was focused entirely on the fact that we were going to war—and that any NATO ally would just have to come along. As a result, Turkey was receiving very mixed signals from the U.S. military.

*"Missteps With Turkey Prove Costly; Diplomatic Debacle Denied U.S. a Strong Northern Thrust in Iraq," Glen Kessler and Philip P. Pan, *Washington Post*, March 28, 2003.

Meanwhile, we ham-handedly tried to buy off the Turks, to the extent that, according to media reports, Turkish officials even began to think they could stop the war if they failed to act on Bush's request to put ninety thousand American troops on Turkish soil.

In my opinion, had we recognized that this ally was between a rock and a hard place, with more than 90 percent of its people against a war, and stopped to think about what we were doing, perhaps we could have brought more countries into the mix and sought wider international approval for our actions.

Instead, we got more people killed, threatened relations with one of our most important allies, and lost credibility in the eyes of the world.

I am reminded of an anecdote from the Clinton years, when we were faced with similar complications involving a European ally in a military context. I was involved in a heated interagency debate about how to handle the situation without damaging relations with the country in question. I attended long and arduous discussions over the relative merits of doing nothing versus offering an incentive to sustain the country's support in a military operation in the Middle East. Dozens of people gathered around a table to debate the wisest response. Some people argued that our ally understood its obligations and didn't need anything more from us. If we gave them incentives, it would have a negative impact. There was a painful back and forth. Others believed that we risked losing their support for this critical peacekeeping measure if we did not do something.

Eventually, someone asked the crucial question: will it make any difference if we do this? Would this country walk away?

The military said no. The State Department was neutral. A

representative of the National Security Council, who later became ambassador to a European country, said he thought it was very important that we offer some incentives. When it came to my turn, I had to say that, realistically, I didn't think it would make any difference. In the end, after an extensive debate, Leon Fuerth, Vice President Al Gore's national security adviser, ruled that it was better to maintain the status quo so as not to insult our ally with what it might see as a blatant bribe. Sometimes the hardest foreign policy decision to take is to do nothing. I have seen little evidence of such subtlety in this administration.

The Bush administration's mishandling of its relationship with France, another important ally, disturbed me no less.

The problems became painfully public in the months before the war. Michèle Alliot-Marie, the French defense minister, had phrased her country's issues more or less like this: what will the impact be on the neighborhood? How can we prevent the country from splitting into three? And how can we prevent Iran from profiting from the conflict and becoming an even greater problem than it already is?

She received no answers, despite the fact that her country had contributed fifty thousand troops to the Gulf War. The Pentagon treated her with contempt. Rumsfeld, Wolfowitz, and Republicans in general had decided the French were perfidious, oil-grabbing apologists for a murderous dictator. By shouting so loudly about the French, they were able to draw attention away from the fact that they had no proper plan for after the war and little evidence about weapons.

Relations were at an all-time low. In January, Rumsfeld had dismissed France and Germany as "Old Europe." Alliot-Marie had retaliated in kind with the words: "We are no longer in the stone age, when whoever had the biggest club would knock the other guy out to steal his mammoth steak. If someone reacts huffily to a reality that he does not like, that is his problem, not ours." We were talking about a war and behaving like bad children.

After the invasion, the British *Sunday Times* unearthed documents from the French foreign ministry that appeared to show the French were briefing the Iraqis on their contacts with the Americans. One was dated just two weeks after the September 11 attacks and was signed by Naji Sabri, the Iraqi foreign minister. It addressed the content of talks between Jacques Chirac and Bush and was based on a briefing by the French ambassador in Baghdad. The French leader had been told that the United States was "100 percent certain" that Bin Laden was to blame for September 11 and that the French embassy believed there was "no intention" to attack Iraq but "matters might change quickly." It also said that Powell and Wolfowitz were discussing a possible military operation, and that the secretary of state opposed it while the deputy secretary of defense supported it.

In intelligence terms, there was nothing startling in these revelations. And it doesn't seem strange to me that the French would have been talking to the Iraqis like this. It is the height of chutzpah to assume we and only we are allowed to act in our national interests in Iraq. The French stayed in Baghdad right up to the day of the attack. They were not trying to tell the Iraqis American military secrets. They were hoping for a delay, one that frankly could have worked to our benefit by making it easier for Arab and other European states to join in the effort in a substantial way. They were trying to persuade them that Saddam was gambling on the reluctance of the United States to go to war, and that he had miscalculated.

--

In September 2004, I got another reminder of the value of working with our allies when I took my last trip to Europe as division chief. I traveled with a man I'll call Jose, who by then had replaced Cofer Black upon his appointment as counterterrorism chief at the State Department. We spent most of the ten days in a certain European capital discussing counterterrorist issues with our local counterparts. It was a great trip and brought back many memories of my years living in Europe, and reinforced my belief that we were headed in the right direction in our cooperation with our European allies.

Until we can accept that a foreign government may disagree with us on very serious issues, but still be an ally against terrorism, we will never achieve the cooperation we need. The jingoistic statements of some members of the Bush administration did not help in this regard. With all of the armchair quarterbacking over how to be a spy in the post-Cold War era that has gone on since 9/11, it is hardly surprising that it seems at times that there is no coherent answer to this conundrum. But the answer is right in front of our noses, as it always has been.

We need to define the real nature and scope of what we are dealing with in the war on terror. We have to move away from the idea that Al Qaeda is some sort of secret government that can be defeated in traditional terms. In Europe, as in the rest of the world, we need to map out the links between groups in as much detail as possible.

Many of the problems I encountered at the end of my career resulted from a clash of opinions on this issue. Elements of the Counterterrorist Center argued that we did not have the luxury of time. I understand and respect their passionate positions on these issues, but I believe strongly that we need to *make* the time, move as quickly as we can and proceed using this approach, because there is no other way. Just as the terrorists give themselves years of patient planning to pull off spectacular attacks, so must we force ourselves to do the painstaking, quiet, secret searching and connecting of dots to prevent them. This of course does not mean that we cross our fingers and hope nothing happens while we work. The effort is by nature cumulative, and in pursuing these sources, we will be more likely to find active terrorist threats as we go. This is the only way we can prevent the type of attacks that occurred in London and Madrid, which I fear are the way of the future. In this regard, one European ally in particular, despite its public opposition to the Iraq intervention, has been exceptionally helpful.

This approach depends on one crucial and elusive thing: trust between allies. Despite our differences on Iraq, despite all the bluster about the cheese-eating surrender monkeys, several close allies had begun to break down some of the barriers before I left the CIA. As Americans, we had to convince our allies that we would not do the one thing they have always feared in these joint operations: use our collaboration to penetrate or manipulate their services. This is an old stumbling block, and we had to work hard to build the idea that 9/11 had created an entirely new way of operating. Instead of storing up information for ourselves, we actually had to share it, tip each other off to what our services were finding out without trying to extract any advantage for ourselves, all in the name of identifying and catching the bad guys before they could kill more people. My old colleagues in the intelligence services around the world will probably shake their heads in disbelief to hear me promoting such an idea. The Americans will say that I've gone soft in my old age, that the Europeans are ineffective. They are wrong. This cooperation actually happened on my watch in Europe, and I believe it can happen again, with political will in the right places.

It may sound obvious. But it is far more than that. It is essential. It is, in my view, the key to passing the test that our enemies have given us. To pass it, we have to abandon our normal operating practices. I would love to reveal all the details of our cooperation with our critical ally, but instead I will describe one of our successes, because I would like to give you the optimistic message that we can succeed when countries work together in a spirit of openness and cooperation—to borrow a phrase a politician might use.

— —

First, I should explain the context for this thinking, from my own experience of trying to crack the Greece-based group 17 November, radical leftists who specialized in bombings and assassinations. One of their first victims, gunned down outside his home on December 23, 1975, was Richard Welch, the chief of station in Athens. The British shared our passion for destroying the group, which killed Stephen Saunders, the British defense attaché in Athens, in June 2000—in retaliation, it said, for his involvement in the Kosovo conflict, which it opposed because of its ties to the Serbs through the Orthodox Christian faith. Our work with the British, and the determination of the victims' families to keep their tragedies in the public eye, played key roles in dismantling 17 November.

But just as crucial was the devotion of a retired senior officer and one Greek American analyst supported by a task force working in Athens. The analyst developed information about this group over many years, but the really hard work was done in the latter part of that period. It took one piece of luck for us, and extremely bad luck for a terrorist, to unravel the entire picture of that organization. On June 29, 2002, Savvas Xiros, an icon painter and member of the group, was nearly killed by the bomb he was planning to plant at the ticketing office in Piraeus, the country's main port near Athens. The Greek authorities tricked him into thinking his comrades inside 17 November had short-fused the bomb. Police quickly found the gun that had been used to kill the British diplomat Stephen Saunders two years before. The injured suspect's brother, Vassilis, was arrested soon after-ward and admitted to killing the brigadier. A third brother, Christodoulos, was also arrested. Fingerprints taken at the site of 17 November arms caches uncovered after the bomb went off prematurely led police to Alexandros Giotopoulos, an economist and the suspected founder of the group. He was swept off the island of Lipsi by a Greek helicopter as he tried to flee on a hydrofoil.

In all, sixteen people were arrested after the failed bombing attempt, leading to a trial and to their conviction in December 2003. It was a bittersweet day for us, since the statute of limita-tions had expired on the murder of Welch, my CIA colleague. But it was a great moment nonetheless to see the people behind the killing or maiming of thirty-two Americans, including five mem-bers of the U.S. mission, lose their liberty. Even though it took three decades to win justice, it was worth the wait.

The 17 November case provided an excellent template for

what I hoped to do had I stayed at my post. The idea was to map out links between suspects across Europe. But our resolve sparked a tug-of-war between working-level desks in the Counterterrorist Center and the European division. Some of the rank-and-file officers were determined to sustain the focus on high-value targets. I strongly believe this is a mistake. We need to map out relationships between militants as best we can to get an idea of what we are facing instead of declaring war on an amorphous global adversary.

The whole Al Qaeda phenomenon is based on personal relationships. The real danger comes when one or two of these guys have undergone operational training. But the majority of the people involved are really very average. You might find them in the side streets of Brussels, or London or Paris, or Berlin; they might have been attacked by racists or right-wingers and suddenly radicalized. If we concentrate only on the monstrous 9/11-type attacks, we run the risk of missing the London-and Madrid-style operations, which in the end are harder to pick up but could have even more impact than 9/11 had.

The anti-apartheid struggle in South Africa gives us an important example in history of how an insurgency succeeds. While few would mourn the passing of the apartheid regime, we can learn from its mistakes in fighting the African National Congress (ANC). For many years, although they could never completely destroy the ANC, the South African government held the upper hand. It was only after the ANC changed tactics that it really became effective. As long as they stuck to big bombings like the Church Street attack, which I experienced, the government was always able to stay one step ahead. What really got the South Africans was when the ANC planners starting giving itinerant laborers from Mozambique and Swaziland bags of small mines and instructing them to drop them in trash cans around Pretoria and Johannesburg. We don't care where you put them, they would say, just as long as the explosions cause panic among the white population. Psychologically, it really shook the South Africans. The police realized they couldn't do anything because the attacks were totally random. The trash-can bombs were far more dangerous than the bigger attacks.

By the same token, September 11 was a collision of overconfidence and bad luck on our country's part and good luck, planning, and discipline on Al Qaeda's. Any intelligence officer who has ever developed a complex plan knows how hard it is to pull off an operation that involves that many people. The more individuals involved, the greater the likelihood that it won't succeed and that someone will do something stupid or lose their nerve. And if we have worked for years to identify the individuals involved in these arenas, there's a good chance we will catch them when they fail, as they often will. Once the terrorists or the instigators in the community who inspire people to militancy are identified, authorities need to move quickly to take them off the street and prevent the attack. This puts demands on both the intelligence and law-enforcement communities and their relations with the moderate members of these communities, but these are steps that have to be taken.

By pooling our resources in Europe, we had one of the biggest coups in the war on terrorism. That was how we and our allies captured a European-born convert to militant Islam and a Middle Eastern man who had plotted an attack on a synagogue that killed Europeans. Local police were unable to hold their suspect, who had been in touch with Khalid Sheikh Mohammed, even though he was arrested after the attack. We feared that if he went to ground in Europe, it would be difficult to pursue prosecution against him. With that in mind, we managed to arrange for him to fly through another allied country where he was wanted for murder and could be detained long enough that he would do no harm. He was sitting comfortably at a transit lounge in a European capital, on his way home from the Middle East, when local authorities arrested him. Two days later his Arab accomplice was arrested in Europe en route to another country where he was reportedly plotting a car bombing. Eventually both men confessed, after the Europeans used classic police interrogation techniques to turn them against each other. Because we had a cooperative effort running in Europe, we were able to arrange an understanding between all sides so that no one got upset.

That is one of the pluses of the bloodthirstiness of our enemy. The blood of victims from at least two European countries flowed side by side after that synagogue bombing. Both men are in jail now, in Europe, and the world is a safer place.

In this context it is worth examining the historically close relationship we have had with one ally in particular—Britain. Our ties with that country have been closer traditionally than with any other, but the relationship has developed over the decades and 9/11 certainly brought it to a new level.

On an operational level, I strongly believe that we need to build similarly close ties with other European allies in the interests of averting terrorist attacks and preventing the proliferation of deadly weapons and agents.

The tie to the UK goes back to the days of Franklin D. Roosevelt, who recognized the need to build an organized intelligence service. Before World War II, our intelligence work was an uncoordinated affair, an omen of some of the problems we see today. Until Roosevelt intervened, the pursuit of information about our enemies abroad was undertaken by various branches of the military, the FBI, the State Department, and even private groups like Pinkerton's National Detective Agency, founded by a man who became famous for foiling a plot to assassinate Abraham Lincoln but who also helped create a federal secret service soon after the U.S. Civil War broke out.

Roosevelt wanted to build an intelligence body to rival Britain's then 100-year-old secret intelligence service, MI6, a goal that I think remains worthwhile, since in some ways we have yet to catch up with our British friends in terms of sophistication, though they of course have the massive advantages of history and size.

For this task, Roosevelt chose Wall Street attorney William Donovan, who had won the Congressional Medal of Honor in World War I. Donovan in turn handpicked a group of young lawyers, businessmen, journalists, scientists, and engineers, mostly drawn from Ivy League schools and the New York scene. He worked with MI6, studied its structure and tradecraft, and used what he learned to set up the Office of Strategic Services in 1942, which after the war became the CIA. Many of the men he recruited became the future leaders of the agency—Allen Dulles, who was named CIA chief in 1953 but resigned over the Bay of Pigs disaster in 1961; Richard Helms, who held the post from 1966 to 1973, after running afoul of Richard Nixon; William Colby, who ran the agency briefly in the mid-1970s; and William Casey, who enjoyed a very close relationship with Ronald Reagan. Again foreshadowing some of the turf wars that still dog our search for a unified intelligence body, the military services opposed

Donovan's plan to merge all the services in the United States, and the State Department argued it should run all peacetime operations. The FBI, meanwhile, wanted to maintain its control of civilian activities.

Donovan's work with Britain's MI6 also laid the foundation for our close ties today. Everything about the way we worked came from the British, from our filing system, terminology, management structure, personnel system, and accounting system to the basics of the way we worked overseas. MI6 also includes the British counterpart to the National Security Agency—the Government Communications Headquarters, which provides signal intelligence to other agencies in the UK and protects the security of national infrastructure and information systems from attacks.

The strength of this historical bond has waxed and waned depending on the personalities involved. Helms and Dulles were great Anglophiles, and the relationship was extremely close in the 1950s. But the case of British double agent Kim Philby, the KGB recruit who served as British liaison with the CIA and the FBI until suspicions arose in the early 1950s, planted seeds of doubt in Washington about the wisdom of sharing intelligence with the UK. Many people in the CIA began to hold back on certain sensitive issues. When MI6 was hit with budget cuts in the 1970s, this reluctance on our part became a particularly bitter pill. Overall, the relationship cooled, though there were warmer moments, for example during the Falklands War, when we provided valuable intelligence to the Thatcher government on Argentine military activity. But our British friends were aware that even at a time of war, we were holding back on some things, and they grew bitter.

Later, during the Cold War, it was impossible not to tread on one another's toes as we both fought for influence on the same turf, for example in Africa, where each country was trying to pursue a limited number of targets. This was straightened out as time passed by an emphasis on building close personal ties and trust. These are key elements of the type of warm cooperation we desperately need with our allies in the war on terrorism. We also must take advantage of the intelligence work our European counterparts can do in this regard and not resort to knee-jerk criticism because we disagree on other matters, for example on the Iraq War.

The point is that it doesn't necessarily take bombs or large armies. It takes collaboration between friends. The success we had with the pair of Al Qaeda militants by working with our European counterparts sent a loud message to Europeans flirting with the idea of converting to militant Islam.

It is these informal connections we need to map—for example, between the two men in the previous story, who not only knew each other but also had connections in at least two European countries. The men behind the Madrid bombings were no different. We knew who some of them were and we were even tracking them, but obviously not closely enough. Some of them had been interrogated or even arrested in the past. The point is that we had the information at our fingertips, and with a clear strategy of agreed cooperation, where countries are allowed to do things quietly, behind the scenes—even breaking their own rules when there is a clear need to do so—then the chances are good we can stay ahead of our enemies.

Because of the fumbling around and knee-jerk overreactions after 9/11, we have lost time, but we have not lost the war. The trouble was that before the attacks, we had insufficient resources.

We had won the Cold War, and people were still figuring out how to fight the new one. The Counterterrorist Center was among the hardest-working offices in the agency, and their officers held strong views, centered mainly on high-value targets. While overseas, I, along with other chiefs in the field, had wanted to expand this targeting, while staying focused on the obvious high-value targets. Then, after the 9/11 attacks, we were bombarded with dollars and ended up creating a giant bureaucracy and a massive military-style operation instead of sticking to what we do well, which is recruiting sources and agents. This actually worked brilliantly in Afghanistan, where we played a key role in the military victory, but left gaps in our picture of the nature of the terrorist threat worldwide.

At the agency, I do not believe we have come to terms with how to divide up the work between the geographical divisions, such as the one I ran, and the issue divisions, such as the Counterterrorist Center. Many people have argued that, since the threat is global, we need to treat it like any other crisis, by going through task forces and special teams set up to handle an individual issue or militant group. But the fact is that the terrorists act locally, planting seeds of future bloodshed in cities all over the world, exploiting issues close to their hearts, and we need to be out on the ground digging up the roots in the émigré communities where they live and work. The real key is remaining flexible and avoiding bureaucratic struggles over operational philosophy. I believe Jose shares this view and hope that those in power support him as he tries to keep people focused on the very real threat and not on internal fussing.

We don't need to change all of our methods. We've already proven that they work. We just need to move our sights to new targets and act quickly to detain the terrorists and the community leaders who often inspire them.

As for our European allies, the administration not only wanted them to do the right thing, but to stand up and shout from the hilltops that they were doing the right thing. You can't have secret diplomacy, or secret intelligence, for that matter, under such circumstances. Elements of the Bush administration developed the view that European personal privacy laws were somehow to blame, forgetting that the Europeans have been dealing with terrorism for years, and that we can learn from their successes and their mistakes. In the 1970s the British, German, French, Italian, and other services had great success against groups ranging from the IRA to the Brigada Rosa by developing sources and informants. Many officers of these services warn that earlier efforts based on questionable legal grounds almost always backfired, with terrorists being set free and new followers drawn to the cause by what they saw as abuse by the authorities.

The point is that the Europeans don't need to drastically change their laws. There is almost always a way around difficulties, and if there isn't, you can invent one. The Europeans are able do a lot of things quietly without the threats to personal privacy found in the Patriot Act. This might mean that occasionally someone has to take a personal stake in the effort—even the president.

In one particular case, whose details I cannot discuss, Tenet and Pavitt wanted to pursue an operation I had proposed to correct a problem that had developed. This was a positive move that was supported even by the Counterterrorist Center, but might have involved Bush holding back information from several of his European counterparts. In the end Tenet was overruled by Rice and Richard Armitage, Powell's deputy. Their concern was that the president and Powell should not be put in such a position. We pointed out that under normal circumstances we supported openness with the allies, but in cases like these we needed to be smart and flexible. We knew the European leaders supported our position but did not want to be put in a position of having to deal with it publicly, involving ambassadors and diplomatic exchanges. The situation was corrected but created a public relations problem that didn't help anyone involved. Not surprisingly, just as we thought, the European officials affected asked privately, and with good-humored frustration, why we did not address the issue quietly, without putting them on the spot.

It was just another example of the insensitivities that have characterized the behavior of the Bush administration when it comes to intelligence, behavior that we saw come to a tragic head with the Iraq War. It all began with Curveball.

Chapter Four†

CURVEBALL RISING

Langley, Virginia. July 2002

I n the summer, the push for intelligence on Iraq's
weapons of mass destruction heated up. Even as we
worked closely with our European allies to catch terrorist
suspects, it became increasingly clear to us all that war was
coming.

It is interesting to note that in May 2005, notes from a meeting
of British prime minister Tony Blair's national security team surfaced in the British *Sunday Times*, just before Blair's reelection.
Had they come out before the war, they would have been explosive.

---

† **Publisher's note:** Interactions with a U.S. ally had to be removed from this
chapter in line with CIA secrecy requirements.

They summarized a visit Sir Richard Dearlove, the head of Britain's foreign service, had made to Washington, in July 2002 and gave a description of a "perceptible shift in attitude" in the United States. Military action was now seen as "inevitable" and would be justified by the conjunction of terrorism and weapons of mass destruction. Stunningly, the notes recorded his analysis that "the intelligence and facts were being fixed around the policy." The National Security Council, according to Dearlove's account, had "no patience" with going the UN route and "no enthusiasm" for publishing material on the Iraqi regime's record. There was little discussion in Washington of the aftermath of a war. Robin Cook, the foreign secretary, said at the meeting described by Dearlove that he would discuss the issue with Powell the following week and that the case for an attack was "thin." Meanwhile the British attorney general said the desire for regime change was no legal basis for military action. He was right. But desire for regime change seemed to be all that was driving the rush to war.

— —

In late 2002 and early 2003, as the war drums beat ever more loudly, two stories were unfolding in parallel that, in retrospect, call into question the urgency of the threat from Iraq which served as the heart of the justification for the bombing of Baghdad. One took place outside Washington, and we will come to that shortly. The other—the case of Curveball, the code name allocated to an Iraqi defector who had turned up in a German refugee camp in 1998 and made startling claims about Saddam's mobile biological weapons laboratories—unfolded at the White House, the Pentagon, the Defense Intelligence Agency, and the

CIA. At the time, I didn't see just how important it would become. In that sense, I can understand why Tenet did not heed the warnings about this man, whose reports underpinned the legal justification for going to war. But he had oversight of the information coming from both sides of the debate and he chose to go along with the White House.

If our job is to provide reliable information for policy makers, then we singularly failed to do so in the case of Iraq. There are many reasons for this, but in my view, the most important one is that the policy was shaping the intelligence and not the other way around. Had these two cases been subjected to cool, dispassionate analysis, Bush would have been forced to wait to build a proper multinational force that could have taken charge of the entire country and avoided much of the mayhem that has ensued since, not to mention the diversion of resources from the war on terrorism. Perhaps even more importantly, I cannot believe the American people would have approved of the war the way they did. They certainly would not have felt they were in imminent danger.

Those who wanted the war the most sought to exaggerate the threat in order to justify it. They may have believed their own hype. But that's how it seemed to me and to many of my colleagues. Our voices were not heard. The more we unearthed evidence suggesting Saddam had no weapons of mass destruction, the more the decision makers believed he was engaged in an elaborate cover-up to conceal his illegal activities, and that we were not digging deep enough.

— —

Sometime in the summer of 2002, the people at the Center for

Weapons Intelligence, Nonproliferation, and Arms Control (WINPAC) were preparing the pre-war National Intelligence Estimate—a report issued by the DCI that makes pronouncements about how the actions and plans of other countries and groups will affect key national security issues. It is supposed to present all sides of the analysis on a given subject. WINPAC started concentrating on Curveball, an old source who claimed that Iraq had tried to evade UN detection of its biological weapons program by making it mobile in 1995. He also claimed to have been present when an accident at a weapons plant killed twelve Iraqis who were operating one of the vehicles. As a result of his reporting, which was only checked properly after the toppling of Saddam, the war, the estimate of October 2002 changed our earlier assessment that Saddam *could* have a mobile biological weapons to describe our "high confidence" that he in fact had one. About 100 of Curveball's reports were disseminated by the Defense Intelligence Agency in 2000 and 2001 despite the fact that the agency did not vet him to ensure he was providing reliable information.

As far back as the summer of 2000, a year before I returned to Washington, people at the CIA had started having doubts about Curveball. The only American officer to have met him before the war discovered he spoke English. His supposed lack of fluency in the language had been one of the reasons the Germans had denied us access to him. He also appeared to have a hangover.

The first I heard of Curveball, whose reporting in any other context was so marginal that it would never have made it to my radar screen, was in the last week of September, when I had my regular meeting with Pavitt to discuss our activities in detail.

It was usually a fairly informal affair, since we talked regularly and were good friends. We chatted as usual about old times and the events of the day, but just as I was about to leave, he asked me to take advantage of any upcoming contact with the German service representatives in Washington and find out whether they would grant us access to the Iraqi defector. I wasn't sure which defector he was talking about but didn't wish to appear stupid, so I said, "Sure, no problem, I'll do it."

I went back to the office and asked the head of central group—let's call her Ava—what Pavitt might have been talking about. She had heard from other colleagues about the focus on Curveball. She looked into it and explained the background about the Defense Intelligence Agency reports. She also explained that he had faded out of focus because the Germans couldn't validate his reporting and had refused to give us access to him.

I arranged a lunch with my German counterpart. As usual, we met at a restaurant in the Georgetown area of Washington, D.C. Being German, he was always on time, and I was always fifteen minutes late. He would be sitting there politely trying not to eye his watch. Invariably my assistant would have called the embassy to say I was running late, but he would always be there before me, and this day was no different.

We exchanged the usual pleasantries, in English because his English is perfect, learned when he was in the military. Then I said, "This Curveball case."

"You know, Tyler, they're never going to let you talk to him," he said.

"Why not?" I asked.

"First off, the guy hates Americans."

"We can send someone who speaks native German," I said, since Curveball, as a nonnative speaker, would not be able to tell the person was not German.

"He's Iraqi. He'll never know the difference."

We both laughed politely.

"Well, just between us," he said, "and I'll deny it if it ever comes out, we have a lot of doubts about this guy. He's a very erratic character. We've had to move him a couple of times. And it's a single source whose reporting can't be validated, and I personally think he could be a fabricator."

Those were his approximate words, apart from the one word I know he used for sure, because it sets alarm bells ringing for any intelligence professional: "fabricator."

In case he had left any doubt, he added: "It's not really worth asking to talk to him."

I took his point on board and said I'd report his views to headquarters. In retrospect, I'd say he had done his job well, trying to prevent tension between our two services over a source whose reporting could not be proven.

I went back to Langley and called Pavitt. "They said he's kinda crazy and, don't let this get around, but Lothar himself thinks he's a fabricator."

"OK. Stay on top of this, though, will you?" he said. "And let WINPAC know."

I called Ava and said she should tell WINPAC that we had asked for access to Curveball and been turned down. "Then find out everything you can about this case," I told her. I had a feeling it wasn't going to go away. Pavitt didn't ask stuff like this out of the blue. There was something there.

So she went to our biological-weapons-analyst friends at WINPAC and told them the bad news. They exploded. "You can't say that!" they said.

A highly acrimonious e-mail exchange began. Ava is pretty

feisty, and her communications with two of the analysts at WINPAC weren't pretty. Another analyst, at the Defense Intelligence Agency, also got involved in the fray. They were so cocky that they forgot to remove Ava's e-mail address when they had some of their nastier exchanges suggesting that she didn't know what she was talking about and that they would be able to talk her around. Unfortunately for them, those e-mails survived and formed part of the sizeable bundle of documents proving that we tried to warn people away from Curveball.

The WINPAC analysts justified their trust in Curveball by saying that his claims were borne out in open source accounts. Yes, Ava responded scathingly, they are, because Curveball can read those open sources just as well as the rest of us. That's why his reporting should not be trusted; he might not have drawn them from firsthand experience and could be making them up.

— —

On December 18 of that year, McLaughlin's executive assistant met Ava to discuss Curveball. It was clear his information was going to be included in a speech making a case for war, though at that time we did not know who was to deliver it. We thought it might be Bush, or Rumsfeld, or Powell. We contacted our Berlin office and asked them to speak to the Germans once more and ask if we could have direct access to the defector. We told them we wanted to use his information in public. Two days later, the Germans turned us down, but said we could use his information as long as we concealed his identity. They also warned us that they could not guarantee that he would not stand up the day after the speech and say it was untrue, because he was erratic, and they emphasized that they could not vouch for his reporting. I knew that along with their professional concern, the Germans were equally worried about the public embarrassment that might ensue if his identity became known, since he was such a shaky source.

On December 19, all hell broke loose, or as loose as it can break in the sober corridors of CIA headquarters, after McLaughlin told his executive assistant to arrange a meeting between the warring factions to discuss Curveball. This brought Ava, McLaughlin's executive assistant, a biological weapons analyst from WINPAC, and a counterproliferation officer together in one room for an ugly exchange. Ava went in guns blazing, explaining in no uncertain terms that Curveball had not been vetted, that the Germans wouldn't let us near him, and that his claims were worthless and could have been built on information available to the public at large. "They looked at me like pigs looking at a wristwatch," Ava later told me, when I asked her if they'd understood the complications of using Curveball.

One of the others at the meeting, a WINPAC analyst, suggested Ava was not qualified to make an assessment of Curveball's knowledge about biological weapons. Ava is not a trained weapons expert, but she is smart enough to know when someone's lying. At that moment she famously uttered one of her more brutal one-liners: "Well, you can kiss my ass in Macy's window." That was not the only time the debate grew heated. I once had to suggest to her that it might not be such a good idea to put "fuck you" in an e-mail. It would be funny if it weren't so tragic.

McLaughlin's executive assistant later said he had looked to the WINPAC analysts for answers and that it was impossible to make an assessment of the German view on his reliability. There was one other human source on whom they were relying, but he had provided a single report and was later found not to be providing firsthand information. Still, the assistant wrote a memo the next day that swept aside Ava's warnings and pronounced Curveball credible.

We did not give up, though. Ava and I met Pavitt and Steve Kappes, the assistant deputy director for operations, to reiterate our concerns about Curveball. But none of us was aware at that point how central a role he was playing, although the people in WINPAC knew, and McLaughlin's office apparently had a hint of it.

In January the issue resurfaced when a draft of a speech appeared in our division. By then we knew that the speech was to be delivered by Powell to the United Nations in an attempt to stiffen the international community's spine for an attack on Iraq. Ava and my executive officer told me about the language that was included from Curveball and we highlighted it for removal.

That was when I decided that the situation was picking up an unstoppable momentum and that I had to talk to McLaughlin directly. To my astonishment, he appeared to have no idea that there were any problems with Curveball. "Oh my! I hope that's not true," he said, after I outlined the issues and said the source was probably a fabricator. It was then that I began to realize that Curveball was central to the case for war.

My fear was confirmed when I said to a colleague at the counterproliferation division that WINPAC must have something else apart from Curveball to back up their case for war. "No," he said. "This is it. This is the smoking gun."

On January 24 we intervened again, after hearing the president himself was planning to include Curveball's intelligence in a speech. We sent a message on Tenet's behalf to our Berlin office asking for transcripts of discussions with Curveball, noting the president's plans. Berlin wrote back two days before the speech and said they were still trying to get the transcripts and pointed out that the Germans themselves had been unable to verify his reporting. It added: "Defer to headquarters but to use information from another liaison service's source whose information cannot be verified on such an important, key topic should take the most serious consideration."

A subsequent message confirmed we were not going to get access to Curveball.

I asked Ava to prepare an e-mail for McLaughlin's executive assistant to highlight all the problems: we were not sure we could find Curveball; he had a history of being uncooperative; if we used his information and his identity leaked out, his family in Iraq could be killed; and that the Germans could not vouch for his reporting, which they believed might have come from open sources.

I learned later that McLaughlin talked to the WINPAC analyst around that time, apparently in response to this e-mail, and received robust reassurances about the reliability of Curveball.

On January 28, 2003, Bush delivered his State of the Union address and included the following words, built on Curveball's claim he had been involved in creating a mobile biological weapons capability:

> From three Iraqi defectors we know that Iraq, in the late 1990s, had several mobile biological weapons labs. These are designed to produce germ warfare agents, and can be moved from place to place to evade inspectors. Saddam Hussein has not disclosed

these facilities. He's given no evidence that he has destroyed them.

The National Intelligence Estimate had also claimed that there were multiple sources for the mobile germ warfare claim. In fact, Curveball had produced scores of reports on this while two other sources produced one report each, so this was a gross misrepresentation. In any event, one of the sources, an individual who was involved in efforts to overthrow Saddam, had in fact been pronounced a fabricator months before. There was also a fourth source, who had also made only one report referring to a mobile weapons capability, but I do not know which of the four Bush was referring to. In any event, it was already known by then that three of the four sources were either fabricators or extremely suspect, and the fourth would later turn out to be a fabricator, too. We were to learn later that bureaucratic failures had led to the failure to flag some of these sources as unreliable, but it has never been explained properly to me why our warnings about Curveball, by far the most important source on this subject, were ignored.

Then, in February, two days before Powell was due to deliver his speech to the United Nations, McLaughlin's assistant e-mailed me saying his boss wanted to touch base again with the Berlin office. Known for his thoroughness, the secretary of state was subjecting his text to close scrutiny, and there was a demand for confirmation of the source's value.

The message was that the leadership wanted to avoid "unwelcome surprises" including Curveball making public statements, press accounts of his credibility, or journalists tracking him down. The assistant asked for the view of our Berlin office on what would happen in the German media after the speech.

Looking back, this e-mail makes clear that there was in fact a genuine concern about Curveball's reliability. I didn't see at the time that the political atmosphere was driving our every decision, and that these concerns would be swept aside.

The committees that have looked into the way intelligence was handled have said there was no politicization of the process. But I disagree. The overwhelming push toward war made it almost impossible for any dissenting voice to affect the direction in which we were headed. The Senate Select Committee on Intelligence report* that was released in July 2004 deemed "harmless" the repeated questioning analysts faced about linking Iraq to the war on terrorism. But there was no doubt in the minds of everyone who worked at the CIA that the administration was headed in one direction and that we were supposed to follow. Had there not been a politicization of the process, how could so much accurate information have been ignored, and so many lies transformed into truth? The intelligence community took the fall, but our leaders set the course.

People were looking for anything that could verify or validate the idea that Saddam might blow us all up in a puff of smoke. Someone, somewhere, remembered the Curveball reporting and resurrected it. WINPAC analysts first started discussing it with CIA management in August 2002, right before the National Intelligence Estimate came out. It now appears that Curveball's reporting fit in well with information obtained from Ahmed Chalabi's Iraqi National Congress (INC), which at the time was still receiving a $350,000 stipend from the Department of Defense.

*"Blair planned Iraq War From Start," Michael Smith, http://intelligence.senate. gov/iraqreport2.pdf.

As an institution, we were ill-prepared to deal with the consequences of being dragged into the Bush administration's rush to war, and its subsequent fight to justify the invasion. The White House took our work and twisted it for its own ends, and Tenet set a tone whereby people knew what he and the White House wanted to hear. We all felt under pressure. The mere fact that our boss was discussing Iraq every day with Bush and his colleagues at the agency made war seem inevitable. The bureaucratic imperative was to prove one's worth by supporting the president's case for war. That is why WINPAC was so passionate in its support for Curveball.

But the warnings about Curveball weren't the only important pieces of information the Bush administration ignored. Perhaps the single most important opportunity we had to avoid a full-blown war without the support of key players in the international community played out in late 2002 and early 2003, when my friend Bill, one of the most experienced case officers the agency has, maintained contacts through a Middle Eastern intermediary with a senior Iraqi source. The public has always been led to believe that all the intelligence available, however poor, suggested Saddam possessed weapons of mass destruction. The public was misled.

Chapter Five†

MISSING PIECE

Langley, Virginia. 2002

I n the fall before the Iraq War, my friend Bill heard from
his contacts in Europe that they had a reliable source, a
senior source inside Saddam's government, who was
giving them surprising insights into the state of the Iraqi
weapons programs.

This source, a very senior official with access to Saddam and
his inner circle, had told our European counterparts through an
intermediary that Saddam's nuclear program was going nowhere,
that his biological weapons were comparable to a kid's science

---

† **Publisher's note:** Many details of the travel by the person named Bill had to
be removed in line with CIA secrecy requirements. The identity of a European
ally also had to be concealed, along with details of our work with that country.

set, and that his chemical agents, having been scattered around the country, represented little more than a nuisance to a sophisticated invading force. In sum, while Iraqi civilians might have grounds to fear Saddam's weapons, American soldiers would have no problem working around them and it was a ridiculous exaggeration to suggest the Iraqi leader was preparing a mushroom cloud for the American people.

Bill knew this intermediary, or go-between, well, and he maintained contact with him right up to the war. I cannot reveal his identity. But the CIA management took him seriously enough that we were authorized to pay him a substantial sum for his information.

Bill's European contacts told him the Iraqi source wanted to defect. But Bill was more interested in having him stay put and provide us with useful inside information. Strangely enough, the decision makers—and, I was told by my colleagues in the group that was handling Iraqi matters, the president—were only interested in him if he was willing to come to the United States and become a tool in the public arena to help justify the war.

When Bill first told me about the Iraqi's information, I was pretty excited, and I called Pavitt, my boss, and Steve Kappes, his deputy. They shared my enthusiasm at the time and agreed it could be an important development. We had been getting hammered for not having good sources in Baghdad. It seemed like an opportunity to get inside the regime like never before.

But Bill had a problem. He didn't really fit headquarters' image of what a senior officer should be. We were of the same rank, and he'd been in for nearly thirty years. But he was rough spoken, old-school, brutally honest in his presentation, and politically incorrect. Despite his deep understanding of Muslim cultures, in which he has spent most of his adult life, he often did not get the credit he deserved for his long experience and abilities in the field.

As intelligence officers, he and I wanted to know what the Iraqi knew. He was the closest thing anyone had to a solid source in Baghdad, and our instincts told us we should use him to the maximum to find out what was going on inside Saddam's regime. Instead, we were forced to wait while officials at the CIA, and by extension the administration, debated whether it was worth pursuing him, even though his information was of immeasurable consequence to the Iraqis, our allies, and us.

The Iraqi had told Bill's European friends—and later told Bill, through the go-between—that Saddam had recently called his close advisers together and asked the man running the nuclear effort when he was going to get his bomb. The nuclear program chief, Jaffar Dhia Jaffar, replied that they were eighteen to twenty-four months away from obtaining a nuclear device—and that was only if and when they obtained fissile material. This meant they were years away from a nuclear capability, and highly unlikely ever to get one. At the very least, we could afford to delay an invasion. Given the fear that gripped the entourage of a man known for killing off his opponents, one might reasonably conclude from this intelligence that Saddam's nuclear chief was actually exaggerating and that the threat from his program was imaginary. Just as Saddam wanted the world to think he would unleash Armageddon on his enemies, it suited Saddam's close advisers to have their leader believe their programs were forging ahead. The strong implication from this Iraqi source's version was that Saddam's deadly arsenal amounted to a Potemkin village. We had destroyed weapons after the Gulf War; the nation was being misled; and we, however unwittingly, were the masters and mistresses of that deception.

The Iraqi also reported that Saddam, having no trust in his army, had given his chemical weapons to various tribal leaders loyal to him. Thus the deadly gases our troops were being trained to anticipate were out of the picture and certainly did not represent a threat to American cities, except in the most far-fetched of circumstances. Moreover, they were not being stored in the type of conditions that would have made them reliable weapons.

Meanwhile, the so-called biological weapons program was amateur, experimental, and extremely small in scale. The Iraqi had no information on the weapons caches Saddam was supposed to have—the deadly weapons of mass murder that were poised to kill us all.

Had we had an opportunity then to follow up on his reporting, as we have since, there would have been time to devise a strategy for after the war, which the United States clearly did not do. With the support of more of our allies, U.S. forces could have fanned out and disarmed the entire population, identified allies on the ground, perhaps have avoided the prison scandals at Abu Ghraib by recruiting properly trained guards instead of allowing catastrophically inexperienced men and women to play out their sick minds in the dark. We could have won over more Arab countries. Who can say how much smaller an insurgency we would have faced if we had taken our time?

Bill took careful steps to ascertain that the intermediary was telling the truth about his contacts with the Iraqi source. Bill, and I, came to believe it would be worth talking directly to the Iraqi himself.

––

I still believe that the militaries of some of our publicly critical allies were making plans to join a later invasion after the UN weapons inspectors had been given more time to complete their work, which would have pushed back the attack by a year. The Bush administration, however, was not willing to wait, and chose to interpret what the Iraqi source was saying not just as an attempt by this European ally to delay the war, but as a treacherous bid to help Saddam prepare for it. It is absolutely correct that some of our publicly critical allies were trying to delay the war. The question is, why? Did they do it because they wanted to embarrass Bush, as his supporters suggest? Or did they believe it was wrong to go to war? Both may be true. But our blind mistrust of this critical ally robbed us of an opportunity to have a real source inside Baghdad, someone who actually knew what was going on, someone who could have given us an insight into Saddam's thinking.

You would never guess it from the public rhetoric, but our ties to our most critical ally on the Iraq War are close. We work well with its internal and external services on counterespionage, terrorism, proliferation, and other issues. However, because of the tensions at the government level, we do see each other as competitors. Each side accuses the other of collecting intelligence on the other.

But 9/11 prompted both of that country's services to work more closely with us—partly in their own interests, of course. Despite the Bush administration's dislike of the country and lingering bitterness in some quarters over the expulsions, we also stepped up our cooperation with them. At the same time our efforts were eased by the fact that the internal and external services were finally cooperating with one another. In the past we always had to choose which service to work with on a given operation because of the gulf between them. Bill deserves a lot of credit for the good relationship we have now, as he took advantage of their concerns about terrorism. That is how he learned about the Iraqi source's reporting to our European ally in the first place.

Perhaps the starkest irony in this story is that behind the scenes, in ways I am not at liberty to describe, this particular European ally has done more than any country to help track the terrorist threat in Europe, where the seeds were sown for the September 11 attacks and the heartbreaking commuter train bombings heralded Spain's exit from Iraq.

Returning to Bill's pre-war efforts, the Europeans who were assisting him in his efforts did not do so in order to aggrandize their leadership—in fact, it is not clear that the top levels of government there even knew about this effort, which was really a result of good relations between the American and European services. This collaboration happened despite—not because of— the differences between our countries' leaderships.

When Bill first learned of the Iraqi's description of Saddam's weaponry, he recorded through official channels the fact that a European source was calling into question the Bush administration's assessment of the Iraqi threat, and followed that up in September 2002 with a trip to Washington, D.C.

What the Iraqi is saying is pretty spectacular, he told the senior official with whom he met. He wanted a chance to vet him properly as a source in order to establish whether he was reliable.

This official's response to Bill was that our "best source"— Curveball—had contradicted this Iraqi's version of reality. Bill told him he needed more time to get to the man, to confront him and find out whether he was willing to defect.

Shortly after that—Bill remembers the date as late September—Pavitt called a meeting in which he ordered people, including the head of the group handling Iraq, to find a way to arrange a face-to-face encounter between Bill and the Iraqi source at a meeting with an Arab government. This would open the door to a direct confrontation with the Iraqi.

Bill flew back to his overseas base and awaited his instructions. Two months later, he had received no response, and sent a cable back to the Iraqi group asking what was going on. The reply came that they were not sure if this was the way they wanted to go.

Bill reminded the group that Pavitt had instructed their chief to set up the meeting. But he heard nothing more about the matter.

Bill says he then demanded a meeting at headquarters. He was baffled by the quality of the responses he was getting from Langley, which he suspected were being written by junior officials with no oversight. The response from the department he was communicating with, as Bill recalls it, was that they didn't have time to read his information because they were briefing the president every day.

Bill won't repeat some of his language in his response, but he questioned how it was possible for them to do their "goddamned" job if they failed to read his output.

The reply, as Bill recalls it, was: "It's time you learned it's not about intelligence anymore. It's about regime change."

The officers involved in this exchange have since been promoted to the running of a major overseas facility.

The story of the Iraqi source does not end there. In December,

Bill had a series of exchanges with the go-between. I know the president heard about this. I do not know whether Bush was briefed again afterward, but I assume that the issue was buried under a slew of discussions about the war. The go-between ran back and forth between Bill and the Iraqi, confirming the details about Saddam's weapons programs. Bill wrote this report up. The Iraqi group was very hesitant about putting it out until we had sustained direct contact with the Iraqi himself and received more information. Given the nature of the reporting, it should have been put out immediately, with appropriate qualifiers; but eventually, after some debate, Bill's report on this official was disseminated. I am not sure how high up it went, but I found out later, during questioning by the presidential commission that issued findings on the intelligence community's knowledge of weapons of mass destruction in March 2005, that the report had been distributed widely. It definitely went to the Iraqi group and to the White House, but there was no feedback—except for an expression of interest in the Iraqi source defecting so they could put him on television.

He was unwilling to do that. "They'll kill my family," he said. He had seen the rough end of Saddam's grip on power, losing at least two members of his family to the regime. The fact that he was in any contact with us at all meant he was already willing to take a risk, and was worth pursuing, but discreetly.

Behind the scenes, our European allies were asking Bill why we were backing ourselves into a corner with the claim that Saddam had weapons of mass destruction, when we all had the same intelligence on the subject and knew that he didn't.

It was a good question, one that Bill could not answer.

After the Iraqi initially rejected the defection idea, there was a deafening silence from the White House. We remained determined to talk to him and to establish whether he was telling the truth. In the spring, in the weeks before the invasion, Bill embarked on a whirlwind world tour, chasing after the Iraqi in an attempt to meet him. I sent him off with the naive comment: "You may be the man who stops the war." I had convinced myself that I would be the one to run into the conference room saying, "There are no weapons of mass destruction!"

Bill set off in the middle of the night after the Iraqi source signaled through the Arab intermediary that he would be at a conference in Asia in late February and open to a meeting. During Bill's journey, which lasted six days and twenty-two hours and covered approximately thirty-five thousand miles, he kept in touch with me by cell phone, growing increasingly exasperated with every stop.

He flew coach class to one Asian country, and from there, to the place where the Iraqi was due to attend the conference. From there, the Iraqi was due to attend talks in the Middle East that were designed to head off the war. There would be ample opportunity for a face-to-face discussion, we thought.

Bill failed to make contact with the source in Asia, so he followed him to the Middle East, arriving there in the dead of night. Bill told me how the poor desk clerk went nuts with him because he had no reservation. I hate to think how terrified the wretched individual must have been as Bill, exhausted after trekking across the globe, responded with all of the substantial fire in his belly that he had been "halfway around the world" and that he should give him a goddamn room. I wonder what the clerk would have thought had he known of Bill's mission.

Bill called me and said he believed the Iraqi was willing to meet him and asked whether he should continue to pursue him, especially since he had by now indicated that he was entertaining the possibility of a defection through a third Middle Eastern country. It would be difficult, because we'd have to get his entire family out simultaneously, but it would be possible.

I called the head of the Near East division. "We just need a couple more days," I told him.

"It's too late. The war's on," he replied. "The next time we'll be seeing him is at a war crimes tribunal."

I called Bill back. "I guess they're really not interested," I said. "I'm sorry. I could have saved you the trip."

"Fine," he replied, his response belying his anger and disappointment. "I'll catch the next plane." I have paraphrased his remarks, which were as I recall a tad more colorful.

It wasn't quite the ending we had in mind. But we shouldn't have been surprised. As Bill finally headed back to base from the Middle East, it dawned on me that it didn't make any difference whether he talked to the Iraqi or not. The books had been cooked, the bets placed. It was insane. I had joined the CIA to stop wars—but not a needless one launched by my very own government.

Chapter Six

MIDNIGHT CALL

Vienna, Virginia. February 4, 2003

I was watching the late-night news in the living room with Linda and Livia when the phone rang. I thought it must be Livy's boyfriend from college—he was the only one who would call at that hour—but when Livy picked up the phone, the caller ID showed "Unknown name, unknown number." She reckoned it would be someone trying to sell us something. She was ready to give some anonymous telemarketer an earful for calling at that time of night.

We were surprised when she said: "It's for you, Dad. It's Mr. Tenet." She was amused by the idea of answering a call from the head of the CIA in her pajamas.

As I sat on the arm of the couch, I had no idea how important this phone call would become. I'm not sure who was there with Tenet, but there was almost an air of comic hysteria in the voices I heard. Tenet needed the number for Dearlove in order to alert him that British intelligence was going to be included in Powell's speech the next day. He didn't keep numbers like that close at hand—that was my job. I asked Tenet to call me back so I could switch to the secure line in the basement.

When I spoke to him again, I gave him the number for the Secret Service representative at the British embassy because I didn't have Dearlove's number at home. I felt like an idiot—I don't like looking disorganized—but Tenet didn't comment on it. "Call me back if you need anything," I said. But I was curious about all the horseplay I could hear in the background, so I asked: "How are you doing? It sounds like you're having a party!"

He said, "We've been up seventy-two hours and we're a little goofy."

Then I decided I had to speak up about Curveball. Despite all my reports and flag-raising to others, it couldn't hurt to mention it to Tenet himself, even if I knew in my heart it was probably a waste of time. After all, Powell was due to speak at 10:30 the following morning.

"Look," I said, "as long as I've got you, and I'm sorry to sort of spring this on you, but make sure you look at the final version of the speech because, you know, there are some problems with the German reporting."

He was distracted and answered with, "Yeah, yeah, yeah, don't worry about it. We are exhausted. I have to go."

—–—

The next morning I arrived at work and had my morning meeting with my deputy, my chief of operations, and my executive officer. As usual, we talked for half an hour and set our agenda for the day. I was looking forward to Powell's speech, though with some trepidation. I double-checked with my assistant—we'll call her Suzy—that she had passed on my suggested edit to the person who was responsible for gathering the amendments to Powell's speech.* She said she had. The intelligence about mobile biological weapons labs provided by Curveball was definitely marked for removal in our version, she said.

At 10:30 A.M., right on cue, Linda called. "Powell's on," she said. I turned to the television screen in my office. There was Powell, with Tenet sitting right behind him, wearing a blue tie. My wife and daughter, both ardent Democrats, were watching at home. They were happy to see him in their party's color. My politics are complicated. I voted for Reagan and for Bush senior, but I really think of myself as apolitical. Having said that, I voted for Al Gore in 2000. It was a strange turn of events, given that Linda and I had both been fans of Reagan when we embarked on our life together in the CIA all those years ago.

On the face of it, Powell gave an impressive performance, with photographs, intercepts of conversations, and a slide show—just what you'd expect from a military man.

Though the speech failed to persuade the Russians, Chinese, and French to back the invasion at the Security Council, it was generally praised. The most respected American official internationally, bar none, stood up before the world to argue that the Iraqis were engaged in a concerted effort to conceal illegal weapons

---

*Link to Powell's presentation: www.state.giv/secretary/former/powell/remarks/2003/17300.htm.

activities from the UN inspectors and the rest of the international community. There was talk of nerve agents, evidence of Saddam's ongoing effort to build a nuclear bomb, the sound of recorded Arab voices discussing things being "evacuated" in an apparent attempt to fool the world. Powell displayed satellite photographs of supposed biological and chemical weapons activities. At one point he talked about anthrax. "Less than a teaspoon of dry anthrax, a little bit—about this amount," he said, holding a glass vial containing a little white powder between his perfectly groomed fingertips. "Less than a teaspoonful of dry anthrax in an envelope shut down the United States Senate in the fall of 2001." That's when his presentation started to fall apart for me. It was embarrassing. The powder he was holding up was not real anthrax.

Then he turned to the claims of Curveball and the other sources on the mobile weapons labs, producing drawings of trucks and rail cars that had supposedly been converted to engage in germ warfare.

"One of the most worrisome things that emerges from the thick intelligence file we have on Iraq's biological weapons is the existence of mobile production facilities used to make biological agents," he said. "Let me take you inside that intelligence file and share with you what we know from eyewitness accounts. We have first-hand descriptions of biological weapons factories on wheels and on rails."

My worst fears were confirmed. Powell, who had spent days locked in a much-publicized debate over what could and could not go into the speech, was standing up sharing the insights of a man who was suspected of having a drinking problem by the only member of the U.S. intelligence community who had ever met him. It was only one small section of the speech, but it was crucial, because it hinted not only at intent, but also at actual capability.

Suzy came rushing in.

"Didn't we take that stuff out?" I said, my heart sinking.

"Yes!" she replied.

"Jeez, maybe it's a misprint? You don't think they made a mistake and gave him the wrong version of the speech? I guess that shows how much influence I have."

In a sense, his speech made no difference. China, France, and Russia remained supportive of giving UN weapons inspectors more time to work in Iraq before authorizing military action. Just a few days later, the chief weapons inspector, Hans Blix, told the Security Council that his colleagues had failed to discover any weapons of mass destruction in Iraq. Mohamed El Baradei, the nuclear chief, told the council that the inspectors had also failed to uncover any evidence that Iraq had resumed its nuclear weapons program, another claim that undermined the administration's claims.

However, Powell's words did change the minds of some Americans. Support for an invasion jumped to 57 percent from 50 percent after his speech, according to a Gallup poll.

From my perspective, the speech was a disaster, though I was not entirely surprised by it. One of my first thoughts was that the Germans were going to hit the ceiling. I had told them I had succeeded in deleting the reference to Curveball, a bureaucratic victory of no small order. But it was done now, and it could not be undone.

The next day I talked to my German contact. "I thought you said it wasn't going to be used?" he said.

I said I was sorry, I had done my best, but there was nothing more I could do. There was no official response from the Germans, but they told my division in Washington and our office in

Berlin that they were disappointed, and that the decision to reveal Curveball's reporting would make their lives difficult. They were concerned for his safety and wondered if they might have to move him elsewhere.

Then I talked to Pavitt. He was equally surprised that Curveball had ended up playing such a prominent role in Powell's speech. I also talked to Bill, who, as I mentioned before, can be blunt—perhaps the result of witnessing seven wars. "We fed them a load of shit," he said. "It's worse than you know," I told him. "I talked to Tenet the night before and told him there were problems with the reporting, but he obviously didn't take it seriously."

We had failed. It was bad enough that we had not prevented the September 11 attacks and we were being blamed for that. Now the nation was about to embark on a war based on intelligence I knew was false, and we would surely be blamed for that, too.

— —

I have to be honest and say that I personally did not read all of Curveball's reports. I was busy at that time trying to work on real terrorism cases. But a simple check of his travel documents disproved one of his key claims—that he had witnessed a deadly biological weapons accident at a time when he was not even in the country.

His most eye-catching allegation revolved around the two supposed mobile biological weapons laboratories, which were actually meant for hydrogen production to fuel weather balloons, as my colleagues in the Iraq Survey Group, who were sent in to complete the assessment of Saddam's weapons programs, later found. The picture of the laboratories in his file looked like a kid's drawing of a truck, so I wasn't surprised.

Finally, 364 days after Powell's speech, on February 4, 2004, Tenet was briefed on the facts that had been unearthed in Iraq, including that Curveball had neglected to mention that he had been fired from the job that supposedly gave him access to sensitive sites and that he had been out of the country on the date he claimed to have witnessed the 1998 accident that killed twelve of his fellow workers.

For all Tenet's decency, I do feel critical of my old boss, even though it's easy to look back now. The truth is that he over-empowered WINPAC. That is the principal reason why I never understood Curveball's prominence until it was too late. Many of us suspected there was no hard intelligence to support the war. But the administration just kept "whistling past the graveyard," as my deputy and I used to say, hoping that our soldiers would get to Iraq and find the weapons of mass destruction, whereupon Curveball and the would-be Iraqi source would become irrelevant. WINPAC analysts said the management of the Directorate of Intelligence shied away from discrediting Curveball because of political concerns.

Tenet was obviously in a tough spot with Powell's speech. A retired senior officer told me that one of Tenet's staff had said that the White House was looking to create an "Adlai Stevenson moment" for the secretary of state. But his presentation was tissue thin compared to the knockout blow delivered by Stevenson, Kennedy's ambassador to the United Nations, in October 1962. Stevenson had been able to produce surveillance photos showing that the Soviet Union was installing nuclear weapons in Cuba despite its protestations of innocence. Sadly, unlike the Cubans, the Iraqi leader did not back down—as any casual observer could have predicted—partly because we had no solid evidence and he apparently didn't believe we would attack him without it.

In March 2004, we finally obtained permission to interview Curveball in person, though we had to pummel the Germans into letting us in. Tenet eventually had to call the head of the German service himself. The Germans tried everything they could think of to avoid a confrontation. "Send us the questions and we'll ask them," they suggested. Finally they gave in, realizing we weren't going to.

Curveball was unable to explain the contradictions we had unearthed, especially his description of a site at Djerf al-Naddaf, where he said the mobile biological labs were kept, and satellite photos that showed a six-foot wall where he said he had seen the labs moving freely back and forth. His reporting was recalled only after one of our best officers worked methodically with him for two weeks, presenting him with evidence that claims he had made could not be true. Eventually it became clear he could not explain the discrepancies. At the end he uttered words to the effect that he had nothing more to say, and he was pronounced a fabricator. To this day his whereabouts are a secret and I am not even aware of his real name.

My critics have asked why I didn't issue what is called a "burn notice" when I first had concerns about Curveball. However, it would have been totally inappropriate to issue a burn notice on the basis of a report from a foreign service that would not allow us access. It would have required a level of certainty that was not available. But that did not make him any more credible. The heated nature of the debate alone should have been enough to prevent us from using his reporting for any serious purpose, without additional confirmation. In fact, as you can see, even after we had clear evidence that he was a fabricator, it took us months to formally withdraw the intelligence he had provided, so I sincerely doubt that I would have been taken seriously had I tried to intervene that way. It seems to me now that I could hardly have made it clearer that Curveball was not to be trusted, but it did not matter. My doubts stood no chance of being heard.

Tenet, the Democrat holdover, was a convenient lightning rod for the administration. No wonder Bush had him stay as long as he did. He did exactly what he needed him to do by backing up his determination to go to war. Rumsfeld's Pentagon was far more powerful than the CIA, which the White House saw as a political tool rather than a place to turn for information. They chose to listen to the Iraqi opposition in exile, Chalabi's INC, with all its wild claims about Saddam, instead of us.

Cheney visited the analysts repeatedly during this period just to make sure they understood how important the job they were doing was. Over at the Pentagon, Wolfowitz and Douglas Feith, the undersecretary of defense for policy, created the Office of Special Plans, staffed it with ideologues loyal to the goal of regime change in Iraq, and used it to push INC reporting to the top without our intervention. This was an unprecedented level of so-called stovepiping of non-CIA sources, which has always existed, but never to such an extent—carrying such credence and with such consequences. The office, they said, was supposed to concentrate on planning for post-war Iraq. History has shown how much planning they did.

— —

As 2002 neared its end, work was under way at the United

Nations to win support for the war. In November, the British reminded us again that they could not go forward without a UN resolution. Around the same time, many of us came to believe that despite their harsh rhetoric, the French would go along with military operations in Iraq if we let the weapons inspectors complete their work. Other countries in the Middle East and Europe, though not Germany, would also join the effort under these circumstances, but it would mean delaying the war by a year.

At headquarters, there did not seem to be the slightest possibility that the administration might entertain the thought of a delay.

Stunningly, as Bush segued quickly from the war on terrorism into the war on Iraq, so did we.

Every day, Tenet held a 5 P.M. briefing that was supposed to help him prepare to brief the president the following day. I considered these sessions a shocking waste of time, packed with pointless posturing. It was all about getting a line in the daily briefing for the next day rather than sharing information. Europe was not a major issue in these briefings, but on those occasions when we were asked to attend, I always sent whoever in my division actually knew the details of the operation I wished to highlight. The worst thing you can do as a division chief is act like you are familiar with all the minutiae. That's how terrible mistakes are made. Tenet used to laugh about my refusal to attend.

So when I turned up for a special session devoted to Iraq in January 2003, he asked jokingly what the hell I was doing there. I was there because I was curious. A 4:15 P.M. Iraq briefing had been added to our daily schedule in late 2002. It meant that the last three hours of Tenet's day were taken up by a meeting. I always thought this was a mistake. It meant we were devoting almost as much exclusive time to a country that had tenuous links, at best, to Al Qaeda, and to a dictator who did not convincingly present a direct threat to the United States, as we were to the threat posed by Islamic militants across the rest of the world.

Tenet always worried he didn't have the whole picture, and wanted to reassure himself that people were telling him everything and not just what they thought he wanted to hear, which is pretty ironic considering that's what he ended up doing with the president.

The meeting was supposed to unearth everything there was to unearth about the subject of Iraq. I walked in and Tenet asked what I was doing there. "Turkey, boss," I said, reminding him that one of my countries was directly affected by the possible war. "I wouldn't be here if I didn't have to be!" he joked. He was pretty irreverent and used to his roll his eyes at me at appropriate points. I think he saw the posturing the same way I did, but he was driven by the urge to prevent another attack happening on his watch and I think by now he had really bought the idea that Iraq was a legitimate target.

I sat in the corner. They went through all the different sources they had on the ground. It struck me at the time that they were talking almost exclusively about sabotage operations planned for the start of hostilities; how the Kurds in the north and the Arabs in the south would blow up railroads with our guys or knock out telephone lines and cell phone networks. They talked about what the Kurds were finding out on scouting missions and discussed details like the problems we were having communicating with agents. I have thought a lot about that meeting, because it suggested that we in fact did have sources in Iraq—not enough, but we had them, sources on the ground who were being used almost exclusively for tactical purposes, trying to locate Saddam and so on. This was really preparation for war, and it happened before Powell's speech.

From my perspective, and I'll admit it wasn't my area, we should have been trying to get a clear picture from our sources about the nature of the threat we faced, using our agents in the classical way, to establish whether there were weapons, rather than solely concentrating on tactical reporting for military purposes. Instead, the people in the Iraqi group who were running the show were looking for buildings to blow up, trooping down to Central Command all the time. There was little discussion of what I viewed as our most important role, collecting reliable reporting that would give us an accurate picture of what the overall situation was in Iraq, how this would affect the need for military action, and what we would face once the initial fighting was over.

While I have huge respect for Tenet, I think one of his weaknesses was that he followed his feelings too much. By taking a personal interest in a given group—first the Counterterrorist Center and later the Iraqi group—he interrupted the chain of command, over-empowering people. The same thing happened at WINPAC. I approve of shortening the distance between an officer in the field and the head of the organization, but in a bureaucracy like the one at headquarters, there has to be an efficient structure in place. Instead, junior people felt like they were reporting directly to him instead of to their supervisors, and lines of communication broke down. The Iraqi group was nominally under the command of the head of the Near East division and the deputy director of operations, but they clearly believed they reported to Tenet and the White House. This was a dangerous trend, because when junior officers feel they have an opportunity to make an impact on top people without checks from intermediate-level staff, they run the risk of being influenced by the desire to make a splash and set aside their own judgment.

———

I felt bad for the Germans when we eventually revealed the depth of Curveball's fabrication. After all, they had always warned us that they could not validate his reporting. There's nothing more irritating than a foreign service coming in and questioning your source, as we did in early 2004.

People were glad to finally get to the bottom of the whole affair. We knew in the backs of our minds that with the Senate Select Committee on Intelligence planning to investigate the data we had on Iraqi weapons, and the Silberman-Robb Commission —which was to report to the president—coming up, things were going to become very interesting for us.

The reaction inside the agency was wrongheaded, if pre-dictable. Despite the communitywide involvement in this fiasco, the Directorate of Operations was slammed—though we were innocent. Tenet announced that new measures must be put in place to insure that this did not happen again. Jami Miscik, the deputy director for intelligence, the chief analyst, delivered a stinging speech in the geodesic dome that serves as the agency's auditorium, after the committee found the National Intelligence Estimate had been wrong. She said the analysts would have to be able to vet our clandestine sources from now on. I disagree with this. It would be the death of good intelligence work, especially given the performance of some of the WINPAC analysts during the entire affair. She also said that people had been misled by multiple source descriptions into thinking that Curveball was more than one person. But that was simply not true. WINPAC had access to all the operational databases at the counterproliferation division, so there were no grounds for confusion. They could easily have checked. The response from the analysts was that they were only using what our directorate had given them. But that wasn't true, either. They had built much of the estimate out of other intelligence, some of it from the INC. But none of these nuances really made it into the headlines. It was the mad, middle-aged, incompetent, sloppy CIA in general and the Directorate of Operations in particular that was to blame for the failure to find weapons of mass destruction.

Parts of Jami's speech found their way into the press, including the front page of the *Washington Post*. In the postmortem, our branch was slammed, while Pavitt, Kappes, and the directorate's leadership were unfairly criticized for their management of prewar intelligence collection. In fact, they were the victims of a flawed policy that made proper intelligence collection difficult if not impossible, since the administration did not want to hear reporting that contradicted their view of the world. Pavitt and Kappes were good officers and decent people, unfairly caught in a very dirty political game. It was the beginning of the end of the agency that I knew.

Chapter Seven

THE SCAPEGOATS

Langley, Virginia. January 2003

I t was a bitter day in the winter before the war. I was depressed about everything that was happening at work. I wasn't sleeping properly. In fact, back in early 2002, when the emphasis began to shift to Iraq, for the first time in my life I had started suffering from insomnia. The aggravation at work carried over into my personal life. I was always coming home and complaining about the tussle over resources I wanted to devote to mapping out terrorist cells in Europe. This was a normal consequence of making the transition from the freedom of an overseas posting back into the bureaucratic soup. But it was compounded by the urgency to find the terrorists I was convinced were living in Europe. It drove me crazy that the people at the Counterterrorist Center kept telling me Europe wasn't a focus of importance, especially since several of the 9/11 hijackers had come through Germany.

I grew grouchy and started staying up late to watch movies in order to take my mind off work. I was gaining weight. Linda and Livy were growing increasingly concerned. I had always said that I felt like a professional baseball player, like I was getting paid for doing exactly what I wanted to do. I loved my job, but if I was unhappy, it made all of the sacrifices my family had made all the more frustrating and regrettable.

I knew that management—Pavitt and Kappes—were taking my concerns seriously. The more I focused on this aspect of the work, the more irritable I became, and the less involved in my home life. Linda and Livy grew more worried. My daughter in particular got homesick as she tried to concentrate on her studies at La Salle University in Philadelphia. To my great surprise, the separation anxiety grew so great that in January 2003, she transferred to George Mason University in order to be closer to home.

That same month, the sleeplessness was taking its toll and I fell ill with the flu. It was a Saturday, and I went with Linda to the little white Methodist church on Kirby Road in McLean, where she did volunteer work. As she dealt with her responsibilities, I was sitting in the last pew, dozing in the sunlight that was coming through the window. The minister came up to say hello. Because I was still under cover, we'd led him to believe that I worked somewhere other than at the CIA. He asked me what I thought was going to happen in Iraq. I was pretty dopey, half asleep. "It's sad," I said. "There's going to be a war, no matter what everyone says, and I'm not sure that we are ready. A lot of Americans and innocent Iraqis who don't need to are going to die."

The minister looked at me, shook his head, and walked away.

——

What was truly galling was that even the leadership of the military, who should have known better, was taking a cavalier attitude.

In February, a friend in the Near East division forwarded to me an e-mail from a colleague who was stationed at that time at Central Command's headquarters in Qatar. Our colleague had witnessed a so-called planning meeting and was sufficiently appalled to describe it to his friends back at headquarters. Tommy Franks, Central Command commander, was in charge. Some poor fellow from the State Department had been assigned to work alongside the military chief, preparing for after the war and considering the diplomatic issues. We were assuming at that time that State would take over the running of Iraq once the military phase was over. This did not happen, much to the shock of our European counterparts. General Franks made clear his disdain for his State Department shadow. While the guy was trying to brief them, he talked, walked around, ate peanuts on one occasion, and even joked around with others at the table. The implication was that post-war planning was irrelevant; that it would be sorted out after the fighting was over.

I remember calling Kappes not long before the war began and saying I had a really bad feeling about it. "A lot of us do," he replied. "We're heading into a murky area we've never been in before, attacking a country where neither we nor our allies have been attacked. We'll just have to do our job." Even if we were dubious about the direction we were taking, it was our responsibility to act in our country's interests, gathering what intelligence we could.

But this sharp former Marine, the assistant deputy director for operations, knew exactly what was coming. "When this is all over," he said, "they're going to blame us."

Now, with all the bad planning behind us, we have few options in Iraq. We've almost passed the point where we can do anything to improve the situation. There was a time when I argued that we should in essence reinvade the country with a proper force and disarm everyone. In fact, that should have been done when we first invaded. The coalition authority turned out to be a disaster not only in conception, but also in practice. We want to be in charge, but we don't want to be responsible for the mess we've made. So it's been terribly easy to blame the CIA, which, let's face it, has been a player in several disastrous episodes in modern American history. But to say the mess in Iraq is the fault of the intelligence community is self-defeating. The intelligence community is part of a government led by this administration.

Now we're stuck with either leaving Iraq, which could herald a disaster of biblical proportions as the country and quite possibly the region descend into civil war, or staying, which will mean that more and more Americans come home in body bags. That is the price of bad planning and failing to treat war as the very last option. In politics, you can make things so by saying it. But you can't apply the logic of a political campaign to international conflict. In the real world, it's different. Cheney can go on television and say, "We've got them where we want them." The forces can say every week that they've caught yet another senior associate of Abu Musab al-Zarqawi. But that won't stop the insurgents carrying right on doing what they're doing. And it won't change the fact that our men and women will continue to fight and die in Iraq every day, unless an Iraqi Gandhi or

Abraham Lincoln emerges from Baghdad's poor Sunni neighbor-hoods. So we must stay on and work as hard as humanly possible to prepare the Iraqi military and government to take over the country and administer it in a way that neither leads to civil war nor destabilizes the region. If nothing else, we must learn the lessons of Iraq and make certain that the next time the potential for military action begins to develop, we act on reporting of a real threat and not as an extension of an academic exercise. The young men and women who bear the ultimate risk, both military and CIA field officers, deserve no less.

The lack of planning spilled over into our operations in Baghdad. In the immediate run-up to the war, as we prepared for the post-invasion phase, we were contemplating an office of fewer than one hundred people. That was in the days when the war's supporters in the administration were still leading us to believe that Iraqis would welcome us with flowers and our troops would be home in no time. Instead, in May 2003 we had to take over the fruitless hunt for weapons of mass destruction and assume responsibility for interrogations of detainees who were considered to have potentially valuable information, a job that should have been done by a police force that did not exist. The demands of a deadly insurgency meant that instead of having a manageable peacetime operation on our hands, we were faced with what amounted to a full-blown war. The only other stations in CIA history that are comparable to the burgeoning Baghdad operation were in Saigon, which at one point reached more than a thousand, and in Bonn at the height of the Cold War. At the last count I am aware of, the Baghdad office was home to several hundred CIA employees and showed no signs of getting any smaller. Needless to say, the operation required highly experienced hands at the helm—and they were not always available, given the pressures of such a dangerous assignment and the small number of people experienced enough to deal with them. It was an additional challenge to have to support the overstretched military there.

It did not help that Rumsfeld and others seemingly never tired of underplaying the size of the threat. His mantra that we were facing the bitter-enders, the thugs and thieves, the dying throes of an insurgency, even as the death toll mounted before our eyes if not always on our television screens, irritated me even after I retired. But even early on in the occupation, the truth was that behind the scenes, the Near East division was already reviewing the Saigon files to see how to address the reality we faced on the ground. Just as there had been before the war, there remained a real divergence between what the Pentagon and the agency were saying. The agency officers were reporting that the insurgency was much more widespread and pervasive than people back home were being encouraged to think.

Just as we were beginning to see the consequences of the bad planning on the ground in Iraq, the manipulations of intelligence that had taken place before the war were coming home to roost.

Some weeks after the war began I was sitting with Mike Sulick, the Vietnam vet, and Buzzy Krongard, the executive director. Pavitt and McLaughlin were down talking to Tenet. Pavitt walked in and said: "They're really upset about those sixteen words. The White House is really angry with George. We sent this memo but they can't find it." He had just been down in Tenet's office and had apparently heard how bewildered Tenet was that he was being blamed for the fact that the president had included an erroneous reference to Saddam's uranium procurement efforts in a key speech earlier that year.

Buzzy said anyone who thought a politician would stay loyal forever was naive. The sad thing was that Tenet had remained a loyal servant of the government; perhaps he was overcompensating for being the lone Democrat holdover from the Clinton administration. It was apparently too much to ask that the loyalty be reciprocated.

Hearing this confirmed for me that the honeymoon was over. The CIA was never going to be the great hero of the post–9/11 era, going forth and catching terrorists. We were going to be the scapegoats.

Tenet fell on his sword for his boss in the summer of 2003, saying in a public statement that it was his fault that Bush had stood up before the nation in the State of the Union address in January and accused Iraq of trying to buy uranium from Africa. It looked like we were not just to blame for the failure to find weapons, but also for the fact that we were now dealing with a bloody and growing resistance movement that had begun in earnest in May, when Bush declared the war was over. It was like watching a car wreck.

I was not involved directly in the story behind those famous "sixteen words" that were spoken by the president but that marked the beginning of the end of Tenet's career at the CIA: "The British government has learned that Saddam Hussein recently sought significant quantities of uranium from Africa." The speech had not been sent to our division for review.

A lot of people thought Tenet would resign immediately after the statement on July 11, in which he said that the "sixteen words should never have been included" in Bush's speech, and that the "CIA should have ensured" they were removed in the vetting process, for which, he said, he was responsible. I was out with the flu again around then, but I was called back in to brief Tenet because he had to give testimony to Congress on the uranium story. I had recently returned from a trip to Europe and had heard the story firsthand. It all revolved around an Italian journalist who had passed on a package of forged documents backing up the supposed uranium procurement attempt to an American embassy official in October 2002, a month after the British government issued its white paper making the claim that ended up in the president's speech. The documents consisted of faked messages and contracts "showing" that Iraq had agreed to buy five hundred tons of yellowcake uranium, a material that could be used to make a nuclear bomb, from Niger.

The deputy head of the counterproliferation division and I met Tenet and his chief of staff in the director's office. I'd never seen him look so down; he looked like the stuffing had been knocked out of him. The counterproliferation officer gave him all the details about the investigation into the uranium allegation, demonstrating that it was false and depressing Tenet still further. The truth was that Tenet had in fact called Stephen Hadley, Rice's deputy, to ask him to remove the uranium report from a presidential speech in October 2002. The reference to the uranium also made no appearance in Powell's speech. But for whatever reason, the allegation resurfaced in the State of the Union speech, and no one took it out. Eleven days after Tenet's statement, Hadley himself acknowledged that he should have removed the words from the presidential address to the nation. But his admission was lost in the hubbub over Tenet's mea culpa.

I don't know exactly why Tenet took the blame. I know his senior advisers felt he was acting as a lightning rod for something that was really the fault of the White House. My theory is that it was clear to him that someone had to take the fall, so he just said what the heck, I am tired of all the whining at the National Security Council, and rather than blame my staff it might as well be me who takes the knock. Perhaps this decision was made in return for a promise that he could stay in charge of the CIA, since he did not quit right away. But I don't know.

It had been widely expected that he would leave when Bush won the 2000 election—he is a Democrat, after all—and it never entirely made sense to me that he stayed on. I believe he was politically seduced in the rush to war and that he failed to create the necessary professional distance between himself as an intelligence expert and the White House and its desire to begin the invasion. He became a part of the policy-making apparatus as a result of being dragged into the inner workings of a White House that behaved as if it was on a constant war footing. In the process he sacrificed the objectivity any intelligence chief must have if he or she is to deliver unwelcome information to the policy makers.

I know he had this distance during the Clinton years. I am aware of a number of instances where he unflinchingly delivered extremely unwelcome pieces of intelligence to the White House.

That's not to say that he lied about his belief that Saddam had weapons of mass destruction. He appeared to believe that wholeheartedly, despite the warnings he received from me and the concerns being raised within the organization he ran. Perhaps, like the administration's leadership, he too was gambling that the weapons would be found. The atmosphere at the time was that as long as we remained certain of our convictions, everything would work out. That approach trickled down from the president.

I doubt I will ever receive a complete explanation for why he stuck to his story about the telephone conversation we had that night before Powell's speech at the United Nations. Perhaps he thought I would be willing to perjure myself by not mentioning it to the Silberman-Robb Commission, and felt that I had betrayed him. I suspect there was some reason why it was important for him to say we spoke at 7 P.M. rather than 11 P.M. I do not know why.

Mostly I feel that we were two good friends and colleagues who accomplished a lot together, until we were set at odds by the manipulations of an administration acting ideologically instead of intelligently.

Tenet may also have been a victim of his own success. I was in the room when he said once after Bush was first elected that he fully expected to be fired. But then he agreed to stay on until they found a replacement, like the good soldier that he is. He spent those months in the run-up to 9/11 trying to attract attention to the looming threat from Al Qaeda. After the attacks, he was able to walk right into the Oval Office with a plan for Afghanistan that caught the president's eye and made the Pentagon look as if it was asleep at the switch. He is an astute politician, and the president immediately liked him. I think he was driven eventually by his desire to stay in his job, at which, under normal circumstances, he excelled. He felt a strong desire to make reforms at the CIA; reforms that most of us agreed were essential.

I know he would have liked to accomplish that goal.

Still, it was clear he bore some portion of the blame for not following up on Curveball, but he was also a victim of poor staff work at the CIA and the National Security Council. I still believe that people at the NSC didn't question the report because it fit so nicely into the president's message. Tenet's share of the blame pales by comparison. Unfortunately, it is all that most people remember.

The Senate Select Committee on Intelligence held the hearing behind closed doors and gave Tenet a pretty hard time. After that, he went on leave for two or three weeks. When he returned, he was back in the driver's seat. The frustrating thing was that we were at war and there were far more important things to be talking about than who was to blame for the sixteen words.

We looked into the forged documents, but we were never really able to figure out exactly what was behind them. I don't buy the conspiracy theories that have erupted since, suggesting that someone in the United States faked the documents in order either to discredit the president or to generate intelligence that would back up the case for war. It would have been far easier just to leak the story to the press. There would have been no need for all the intrigue, with the documents handed to the Italian journalist and the forging of the original claims. On the basis of conversations I have had with friends in European services since this scandal erupted, I believe there is truth to the allegation that Saddam wanted to acquire uranium, but the effort never reached the level of success suggested in the documents. With my three decades of experience in this business, I believe the explanation is simpler and far less dramatic than people think: someone at the Niger embassy in Rome made up the documents and passed them on through contacts in Italy in an effort to make some money from a variety of intelligence services. In confirmation of the law of unintended consequences, the whole matter ended up generating confusing diplomatic correspondence and was eventually repeated in the British dossier mentioned in Bush's speech, presumably after being handed to my counterparts in London.

From the point of view of the White House, Tenet's mea culpa served its purpose by drawing attention away from the wider question of whether the president had misled the nation, as it prepared for Bush's 2004 reelection campaign. But the White House wouldn't get off so easily. It also had to contend with a rare public attack from a prominent diplomat, Joseph Wilson, who had been the acting ambassador to Baghdad when Saddam invaded Kuwait and who had been sent on a mission to Niger in February 2002 to investigate the uranium claim. His wife, Valerie Plame, an undercover CIA officer working on weapons issues, had reportedly suggested he would be well qualified to look into the matter because he knew the former prime minister of Niger.

In July 2003, just five days before Tenet's mea culpa, Wilson published an editorial in the *New York Times* saying the Bush administration had twisted intelligence to exaggerate the threat from Iraq. His discussions with the former prime minister had produced no indications that any uranium sale might have been attempted. This caused a media firestorm and led to a strange turn of events that hit close to home for me as an agency man.

Karl Rove, Bush's closest adviser and strategist, played a central role in the administration's subsequent effort to discredit Wilson. In July 2005, a *Time* magazine reporter was forced by an independent prosecutor to reveal that Rove had told him that Wilson's wife was a CIA officer, an act that in some contexts can be illegal, though currently no charges have been filed against Rove. His alleged discussion of the profession of Wilson's spouse may have been intended to discredit Wilson's criticisms of the war; the implication was that Wilson's analysis should be taken with a grain of salt because he was married to an occupant of that nest of liberals over at the CIA, which was no doubt keen to hit back at the White House after being blamed for the mishandling of intelligence in the run-up to the war and before 9/11.

Whatever the outcome of the grand jury investigation under way at the time of this writing, the revelations about the administration's role in the Plame case show just how dangerous it can be when an administration behaves as if it is permanently on an election footing. Rove is really a campaign manager, and yet he was intimately involved in the planning for and justifying of the war, to the extent that he saw it as his job to discredit its critics. While I do not know the full facts of the Plame case, it is clear he was involved in a way he should not have been. At some point an administration has to make a break with campaign mode and move into governance. I believe the administration's decision to reveal Plame's profession will leave a black mark on this president's legacy.

Some people have suggested that since Plame was at the end of her career, married to such a prominent figure and back in Washington, it didn't matter that her cover was blown since she could no longer be used to run covert operations to any great extent. That is not the point. Whether the time had come to go public with her name was not a decision for Rove or any other politician to make. He hadn't earned that right. Cover is a very fragile thing and it only works as well as you work at it. Revealing her identity was a kick in the teeth to all the men and women around the world desperately trying to maintain their anonymity.

I served under that type of cover for many years of my life, going through all the irritations of pretending to be someone I wasn't. Every time something bad happened, I had to worry about getting caught and my family getting in trouble. Plame will never again be able to go abroad, working in secret. This revelation could have immeasurable consequences for all the people whose lives she touched over the years.

Other intelligence services and governments may come to

suspect someone is a CIA agent, but unless someone confirms it, they will never know for sure. When I was under cover, my real name with my true identity appeared three times outside CIA channels: in an Indian book about the CIA in Africa that was intended for a local audience; in an Austrian magazine piece; and in a German book written by a former Stasi officer that as far as I know was never translated into English. I did not have to reveal my identity, because we never confirmed the reports. I was able to continue my career. While Plame was out schlepping around the world, taking risks every day, Rove, Libby, and the rest of the political operatives in Washington were sitting safely on home turf, benefiting from her courage.

This lack of regard for Plame's cover confirms for me that this administration is unable to separate campaigning from wise policy decisions. It was willing to sacrifice the CIA, its director and its officers, and the agency's ability to protect the safety of the American people, for political interests. That is not something I have seen an administration do before.

—

We could sense change was coming, and that it wouldn't be for the good. The shock waves going through my workplace also hit my wife and daughter, who had always been part of the CIA family—how else could we sustain my cover? I blamed myself.

For the first time, Linda, who had been supportive through the hardest times of my career abroad, felt she had to let me know I was allowing my work to affect my relationships with her and Livy, as well as with my sister, and with my mother, who was seriously ill with heart failure. Funnily enough, the one person at work who really lent a sympathetic ear during this period, as you will soon read, was Tenet. It was odd, since he was playing a role in creating the atmosphere that caused the problem. It was all very confusing and frustrating. For the first time in my long career, I began to think about retiring.

With every passing week, as weapons continued not to be found in Iraq, my wife, a Reagan Republican turned Democrat, who had given up her life first to the CIA to serve her country and then to be at my side as I did, grew increasingly angry. When Bush, Rice, and the others started saying their actions were based on the intelligence reporting, that they had only presented the intelligence they were given by the CIA, our sense of betrayal grew deeper. She had heard me say that we had reported that Saddam had no such weapons, and that it just wasn't what the decision makers wanted to see. She felt that after everything we had given to the agency, all those years in the shadows, in war zones, in danger, it was a shame to see the agency being unfairly embarrassed, to see the Directorate of Operations being made the scapegoat for a policy problem.

Linda had been such a devout Republican that in 1980 she took leave to drive home and cast a vote for Reagan. My wife and I were raised Republicans. In 2004, many in Linda's family could not understand why she was campaigning for Kerry. We tried to avoid political discussions with our families. Linda's mother was sad when Bush senior failed to get reelected. She could not now understand why Linda would support Kerry. Meanwhile we were still under cover, which was good for Linda, in a way, because many Democrats retain deep suspicions of the CIA. Linda, who comes from a very Republican area in Carlisle, Pennsylvania, has only recently begun to tell any of her friends what my real job was.

Eighteen years later, she had become a serious Democrat, a conviction that only grew in strength with the war. Her views, to her great sadness, put her at odds with her conservative parents, who supported the war wholeheartedly. Like most Americans, judging by the elections, my in-laws could not believe that the government would invade Iraq without reliable intelligence, yet they wanted to support me. They were torn.

Many CIA families faced this conflict at that time. We had always believed that patriotic citizens were supposed to support their president at war. But, like many of my colleagues, knowing what we did, I found this increasingly difficult to do. Perhaps Bush was driven by good intentions—one could argue. But what he did was wrong, and we went to work every day on our president's behalf knowing that, given time to build a real coalition, we could have removed Saddam for any one of the many crimes he had committed. This would have removed the dictator and left our country and the world safer. In squandering their success in maneuvering the UN into a position to support action, the administration set the stage for the lonely struggle we now face.

—— ——

In the summer of 2003, things became more bearable because Livy was working as an intern at headquarters. It was a special time, as we drove to work together and sometimes had lunch. She quickly came to understand the complexities of government, and I'm not sure I like what she saw.

In our conversations, it was also clear that she and my wife, brimming with life, full of enthusiasm, and always determined to do the right thing, wanted me to retire so I could be happier. At times, they sounded like advocates for the American Association of Retired Persons. This only confirmed my feelings, but I also felt there was still work to do, that all was not lost.

After all, I had personally been involved in a number of successful operations over the years with a number of administrations, regardless of their political orientation.

Chapter Eight†

PRESIDENTIAL
PREROGATIVES

Washington, D.C. Late 1970s

A llow me to take a detour here and provide some context for what you've read so far, and for what you are
about to read. As an intelligence officer with nearly
three decades' experience serving in Africa, Europe, and Washington, my experiences of life under previous administrations
obviously inform my analysis of the current one. So it is useful to
recall some of those times. I want you to understand why I feel
so strongly that this administration has compromised the work
of this nation's intelligence community like none before.

† **Publisher's note:** A number of details about Tyler Drumheller's foreign assignments had to be removed in line with CIA secrecy requirements.

When I was lower down on the ladder or removed from the Washington scene on overseas assignments, it is true that I had less direct experience of the administrations and less contact with their key players than I did once I had assumed senior management roles under Clinton and the second President Bush. But in the case of Reagan, I was intimately involved in cases that were of extraordinary importance to the White House because of the Cold War context, and developed a clear picture of how my reporting was being received at home base.

Nor did I exist in a vacuum during the administrations of Jimmy Carter and the first President Bush. My fellow intelligence officers and I often discussed the prevailing political winds back home, no matter where we happened to be on the globe, and wherever we stood on the totem pole. So I have well-informed views of how the relationship between the intelligence community and politicians has developed over the years.

There have been many upheavals since I first reported for duty, which was in the aftermath of Watergate, and the hearings on Capitol Hill held by Frank Church, the Idaho Democrat who called the agency a "rogue elephant on a rampage." After Church, clearer lines were drawn on what we could and could not do, which was a good thing, after the disastrous plots to assassinate Fidel Castro and Patrice Lumumba of Congo.

When Stansfield Turner came in as director of the CIA under Carter, he fired many hundreds of people as a direct reaction to the Church hearings on a day known as the Halloween Massacre, October 31, 1977. Among the terminated were many senior officers, and along with them went experience and institutional memory. This purging habit is one we have yet to break (as we will soon see with Porter Goss), but in my view, it must end if we are to get serious about using the intelligence community as a weapon against terrorism.

Despite the turmoil experienced by the agency at the time, I was inspired by Henry Kissinger's back-channel communications with China. So when my Chinese professor, an old man who had fled his homeland in 1949, pulled me aside after language studies class at Georgetown University, he quickly hooked me with his prediction that I would make "a better spy than a professor."

Like me, the CIA was itself embarking on a new era. Relations with Carter had remained mired in controversy to the end of his administration, especially over the botched efforts to end the hostage crisis at the embassy in Iran. On November 4, 1979, militant students—responding to a decision by Carter to allow the deposed Shah to enter the United States for cancer treatment—seized sixty-six Americans, thirteen of whom were freed over time. The rest were freed 444 days later, the day Reagan took office. Before then, however, a hapless rescue mission, called Desert One, took place on April 24, 1980, and it ended in disaster, with the bodies of eight Americans and three stricken helicopters left behind. Carter personally took full blame the next day, to his credit, though it did not diminish the contempt in which he was held by some of the old guard at the agency at the time. (I don't think I need to point out the contrast with the current president's unwillingness to accept any responsibility for certain of his actions.) The role the CIA played in Desert One was kept secret for years.

From my perspective, as a young man embarking on his life as a spy, it seemed that there was a sense of depression and hopelessness at the failure of the Desert One raid. Morale had already plummeted after Watergate and the Church hearings, and now the agency really seemed adrift, unable to address many of the issues of the day.

Such was the anger of senior CIA officers that when Turner held his farewell reception before leaving the post in January 1981, scarcely any of them turned up. His farewell reception was a simple affair held in a meeting room on the first floor of head-quarters. Turner and his wife stood on a small stage, and people passed by, shaking hands. I was one of the many trainees to attend, along with junior officers, and I remember thinking he looked pale and wan. He shook my hand and asked if I was a career trainee. When I said yes, he replied that his efforts to reor-ganize the agency had been for my generation. I felt sad and uncomfortable, and wondered how I would handle my own last day, whenever that would come.

There was a sense that the agency had been downgraded and blamed for the sins of the Cold War, and there was a terrific hos-tility toward the president from some of the senior ranks. I wouldn't blame Carter personally for the CIA's slide at the time, but he did little to boost morale. Still, I had no sense that there was a blurring of lines between the agency's operational role and the role of the policy makers, who seemed far away from our work. I sensed we were able to report what we found without political pressure.

(As I've shown, I believe President Bush became too involved in the intelligence process, through the office of his vice presi-dent and through the National Security Council, which was the most political of my lifetime. That was how it seemed to me on the occasions when I briefed Rice, with her well-lit corner office in the West Wing, surrounded by windows and sports memora-bilia. She was very polite, but she was focused primarily on the political aspect of operations. It was a far cry from the days of Colin Powell, when he was Reagan's national security adviser, and Brent Scowcroft, who served Bush senior. They saw their role as coordinating national security and keeping the president informed, and getting his input only on final decisions.

Nowadays, the agency is at a turning point similar to the one it faced after Carter, and at the end of the Cold War, as it struggles to define its relevancy in the new world of terrorist threats. The biggest difference now is that we are facing the added challenge of fighting off abuse and being made scapegoats by our political masters. It was different when I first joined. I remember talking to a chief of an African branch, my first boss in Washington, who drilled it into me that it was my job to go out and collect information and advise the White House, not to be responsive to their preconceptions, as was the case on Iraq.)

So when I arrived in Africa on my first overseas assignment, in September 1981, I was filled with a sense that I could make a difference, and I was not to be disappointed.

In many senses, we were stepping into the lion's den. There had been a series of expulsions of U.S. spies from Africa, so the officer who was supposed to take over as deputy chief of the local office had been banished and couldn't return to the continent. This meant that Cofer Black moved up to fill his shoes, and there was an opening in his old slot in Lusaka. They asked me fill it in March 1981, just two months after Reagan took office, heralding the beginning of what we all thought would be a golden age for the agency. Reagan appointed William Casey, who led an aggressive and enthusiastic expansion of the agency, albeit at one of the most controversial times of its history. By sheer force of personality, he improved morale and gave us a sense of being involved in the great events of the day.

With Casey as director, it was like Dickens. It was the best of times and the worst of times. The good news was that thanks to his understanding of espionage based on his World War II experiences—he ran the Allies' espionage operations behind German lines—and his relationship with Reagan, we were allowed to be extremely aggressive in pursuing the issues of the Cold War. The bad news was that because of his relationship with Reagan, we often felt that we could do anything we wanted. And did. We got caught up in policy and ended up right in the heart of the Iran-Contra affair. That was the first time I had been around long enough to look at the covert branch of the agency, the Directorate of Operations, as a whole, instead of life in my particular office. I realized that as Mike Sulick, who'd sat behind me in our induction classes all those years ago and remains a firm friend, often says, whenever we start getting away from what we are really supposed to do—collect intelligence—and get into the great game of nation building, we always seem to get into trouble. Looking back, this period foreshadowed the issues we face today. Yet, even in those heady days, the level of political interference was minimal compared to the current atmosphere.

For in Africa, despite the Reagan administration's strong ideological bent, I felt that my direction came from my local boss. We reported what we saw. There was nothing coming from Washington except clear direction of what our goals were. Nor did I get the sense that we had to handle our reports to the White House with kid gloves, like with Cheney. What I saw and what filtered down to me was that we did not have to be careful about what we collected or fear conflicts with the leadership's views.

So when Reagan won reelection in 1984, and Pavitt and I were serving side by side in the African division at Langley, we were happy. I remember saying to Pavitt that we should enjoy Reagan's support while it lasted.

With all my memories of those years, the bombs and the close shaves and the colleagues lost, it really irritates me to hear members of Congress go on about how risk averse we have supposedly become.

Africa was pretty safe, but even there we faced threats every day that most Americans only have nightmares about. I find myself remembering the car bomb left by the military wing of the African National Congress that nearly killed me just days after we arrived in South Africa. It went off just moments after I passed by, sending bodies, limbs, and flesh flying through the air. I remember Linda driving across the open landscape between two African cities with our daughter in the backseat to drop me off or pick me up from agent meetings without blowing my cover. I remember the fear she had to live with when I would take off on some secret mission somewhere, never exactly sure when, or whether, I would return.

Africa was really a classic Cold War assignment, and it is a good example of how things used to be before politics and members of Congress on one of the dozens of committees that have oversight roles started to get too involved in our work. The fact is that it is only by experiencing the world of espionage that you can develop a sophisticated view of how to improve it. Everyone starts out with misconceptions that can be dangerous, and the current crop of congressional staffers who have come in on Goss's coattails appear to be no exception to that rule.

Things were simpler in those days. The policies were not

always right, but we knew what they were, and leaders like Reagan made it clear from day one what we were supposed to do. He wanted to confront the Soviets all around the world where they had established military presences, to keep them engaged and off balance. Each division affected by this policy—including Africa—was allowed to work with support but limited interference from the director's office.

Since then the Directorate of Operations, which is the heart of the agency, has become the whipping boy. The truth is that without the clandestine service, in my admittedly rather prejudiced view, the CIA would basically be a rather small think tank. Without it, the analysts would have nothing out of the ordinary to analyze, the technical experts would have no one to invent for, and human resources would be twiddling their thumbs with no double agents to unearth and fewer eccentric individuals to manage.

It is sometimes hard to believe that the agency, which employs tens of thousands of people full-time, has only been in existence since 1947, considering the vast history it has generated. Truman was responsible for signing the National Security Act that formally created the CIA, a law that also formed the Department of Defense out of the Navy and the Department of War, created a separate air force, and founded the National Security Council. It made the head of the CIA responsible for protecting intelligence sources and methods, and it is the reason why you will find no such details in this book. A subsequent act guarded the agency's requirement for budgetary secrecy, another area I cannot go into.

The CIA's goals are the same as they were back in 1944, when Roosevelt first called for a unified organization under presidential control that would procure intelligence, provide guidance on it, determine the nation's intelligence objectives, and bring together all the data gathered by the various government agencies involved in this area.

The structure is also essentially the same as it has always been, with its work divided into four directorates: Administration, which manages the agency staff and hunts for moles; Intelligence, the analytical branch; Operations, or the spies; and Science and Technology, which runs the satellites and invents and develops the tools of our profession. Our directorate is divided into six geographical divisions and several specialized departments that vary from time to time.

The big difference between the past and now is the vast web of special assistants and staff that seem to jam up the structure, a phenomenon that first developed after Iran-Contra, picked up speed after double agent Aldrich Ames was convicted of spying for the Soviet Union, and has reached an absurd height with the advent of Goss as CIA chief.

In the 1950s and even up to the 1980s, there were brilliant analysts to be found at the agency. That was in the days when their salaries matched our country's expectations of them. The British used to come to us for a better understanding of Ireland because we had arguably the world's smartest analyst of that subject. But the uncomfortable truth is that being a CIA analyst is no longer a high-paying job compared to the openings available for smart people in the private sector. This is a growing problem that has not fully been addressed despite the millions that have been thrown into intelligence work since 9/11. This state of affairs has led to a less experienced analytical corps who tend to be more susceptible to political pressure from their consumers, including the White House. In Europe we were very lucky since our chief analyst was one of the brightest and most experienced among them, and had done a couple of tours abroad. But that is not always the case.

As young officers, we felt connected to the policy but not driven by it. Of course this was partly because we were fighting the Soviet Union, an unambiguous enemy. But there is absolutely no reason why the Bush administration could not have set clear policies in the war on terrorism and achieved the same kind of atmosphere, where the policy was clear and our goals were set. Instead, more than three years after the attacks, we were just beginning to make some of the necessary changes in order to clarify who our enemy really is.

There was a lot of passion in the anti-Soviet days, but there was also a professional detachment that I have not detected in our leadership since September 11. There was a feeling that we knew what the director, and by extension, the president, wanted, and it was no more complicated than to go out, collect intelligence, and report back; they would take it from there. The Bush administration knew the answer to its questions about Saddam's weapons of mass destruction in advance. While the Reagan administration also became more ideological as it got deeper into covert actions—the Iran-Contra affair is the obvious case in point—our work in Africa was an illustration of how Reagan, for all his ideology, let us do our jobs.

I arrived in another African country in 1983 to begin what was probably my best assignment, professionally speaking. I handled a number of senior sources and obtained extremely sensitive information, notably on the country's nuclear program. I knew that my work was having an impact in Washington. Reagan, whose apparent goodwill for the anti-communist policies of the white

South African government was well known, probably didn't want to hear the things I was reporting. But it never even occurred to me to wonder if I was hurting my career by producing intelligence showing that the situation was far more complicated than a simple struggle between the government and the ANC, which received operational support from nonaligned and Soviet bloc countries. All I knew was that I had excellent sources and that the reports were being read. No one was telling us we were a bunch of liberal anti-apartheid activists.

The U.S. mission was roughly divided between a passionately anti-apartheid camp and a group that regarded the ANC campaign as a problem of outside agitators rather than a grassroots rebellion against white rule. Our own civil war history obviously played a role in that. We did have one little dustup with Congress, when Senator Edward Kennedy came to visit. Afterward, one of his staffers gave an interview saying the embassy was staffed by pro-apartheid ideologues. That hurt a bit, but I didn't really pay much attention. Given that my reporting was leading to uncomfortable conclusions about the apartheid government and no one was punishing me for it—in fact, they were encouraging me to stay longer—we clearly must have been doing something right if we were simultaneously managing to annoy a liberal like Kennedy. It was a dangerous posting, but a successful one for all that.

We had operational successes, most importantly regarding Pretoria's nuclear capability. My sources collectively provided incontrovertible evidence that the apartheid government had in fact tested a nuclear bomb in the south Atlantic in 1979, and that they had developed a delivery system with assistance from the Israelis. A huge debate had gone on within the administration about whether South Africa really had a proper nuclear program. Some people believed it was impossible, while others knew they could only have done it with help from Israel and didn't want to face that. Still others really wanted to believe it because they loathed apartheid. The Carter administration had decided to ignore the scientists who were telling them there had been a test on their watch. All I knew was that it was my job to find out what was really going on behind the scenes so the policy makers could sort out the mess.

So we milked our sources for information and also gathered our own data to try to get a picture of how advanced they were in their enrichment of uranium. We found imaginative—and not always entirely orthodox—ways to conduct scientific analyses.

My sources confirmed our suspicions (which South Africa would not admit to publicly until 1997) of not only their capability but also their targets and a highly accurate delivery system using gliders. The frightening aspect of this was South Africa's lack of a plan for the system, originally developed to counter a Soviet attack and now just sitting there waiting for emotions to reach boiling point. This reporting went back to Washington, and even though it was doubtlessly not what Reagan wanted to hear, it made a huge and positive impact on my career.

On another front, I started getting reporting from government and military sources that there was a plan to manipulate U.S. policy and target certain people who were sympathetic to them, including a senior person in the embassy. Through these sources, we learned that the government was covering up attacks in Angola by bombing the open landscape elsewhere to distract us. Headquarters was initially reluctant to hear this reporting. The cables would come back asking if we were sure of our ground, if we had given polygraphs to our contacts, and so on. Then we started to get the information on the nuclear program. We had limited senior sources in the whole country, but that was all we needed to paint a complete picture of what was going on.

Reagan never dropped his opposition to sanctions against South Africa, but there is no question that our reporting on the advanced nature of the country's nuclear program, its manipulations of U.S. policy, and its tireless attempts to assassinate its enemies, which I also helped uncover, provided policy makers back home with an alternative view of the situation. We fell behind the international curve, but we did not veto the French resolution at the UN that called for voluntary sanctions in 1985; we did ban the currency; we did send a black ambassador to Pretoria; and we did eventually end the much-criticized policy of constructive engagement with South Africa that Reagan introduced on entering the Oval Office. Reagan may have gone to his grave with his ideology intact. He stood in the way of wider sanctions and drew accusations of racism from Desmond Tutu. But all of these political and diplomatic machinations didn't stop us from doing our jobs. Our information, obviously in concert with all the other reporting that was going on at the time, the pressure in Washington, and the clamor for action around the world, helped policy makers see that there had to be more to our position than fighting communism in Africa.

It emerged from our reports that the South Africans were frantically playing the anticommunism card while shoring up their regime. They were very creative, and were pursuing development of a weapons program that could have turned an odious regime into a truly dangerous superpower. Washington began to see that our relations with the rest of the world were suffering from our perceived support for the apartheid government. I had a real sense I was accomplishing something. It was becoming very clear that the South Africans had no intention of creating a one-man, one-vote society. They were just playing for time, figuring out how to keep control.

—–

In the mid-1980s, when the debate was raging over Reagan's policy of persuasion rather than coercion against apartheid, I found out that the South Africans were planning an attack on an ANC safe house, I think in Lesotho. As I remember it, Chester Crocker, the assistant secretary of state for African affairs and Reagan's enforcer of constructive engagement, raised the issue with Pik Botha, the foreign minister. "I know you're planning to do this," he said. "Don't." Afterward, Botha was reported to have angrily told his aides: "The Americans know more about what is going on than I do."

Crocker was quite conservative. He and Reagan clearly believed with some conviction that sanctions were not the way to go and that the South Africans deserved some time to dismantle a regime that most of the rest of the world wanted done away with immediately.

Reagan, in the end, when confronted with what the South Africans were truly like, did nothing to stop reforms beginning to take root in the country. After the first President Bush was inaugurated in 1989, we started making more public displays of our opposition to apartheid rule.

There seemed to be an organic nature to Reagan's South Africa policy, however intransigent he may have been. His African policy, while flawed in many respects, was clear. Our goal was to diminish Soviet influence, to drive the Cubans out of Angola. We ultimately left the country to its own devices, didn't move their land mines, and created fighting forces armed to the teeth that continued to pursue a civil war that raged until 2002. But we did help bring about an end to Soviet involvement in Africa and almost completely destroyed their influence on the continent.

The current administration clearly tried to take a leaf out of Reagan's book by creating an "axis of evil" comprising Iran, Iraq, and North Korea. It was pretty easy to convince people that the Soviet Union was an evil regime armed to the teeth with nuclear weapons, because it was. The problem in Iraq was that they never properly defined the policy, beyond saying "Saddam is bad" and "We must spread freedom." They have helped create a policy vacuum by shunning internal critics and turning a deaf ear to voices and reports that contradicted their beliefs.

——

Before Iraq, my work on the Angolan conflict in Africa, Washington, and later Europe, where we arrived in August 1988, five months before George Herbert Walker Bush took office, was perhaps one of the most paradoxical experiences of my career.

It is depressing to me to see that the Bush administration appears not to have learned the hard lesson of this war: when you start down this road of military entanglement, there's no turning back, and there will be no one to tell you exactly what will happen next.

While it is perfectly easy to understand why the Reagan administration threw itself into Angola, this cautionary tale illustrates how careful you have to be if you start seeing things in black-and-white terms. It behooves us in such situations to be cautious and pragmatic and avoid seeing things in strictly emotional or ideological terms. Having said that, Reagan did seem to be able to compartmentalize his opposition to racism and his view of the white South African government as stalwart anticommunist allies and the ANC as a communist front organization, especially as most of its leaders really did have some contact with the Soviet Union.

Under Reagan and the first President Bush, our policy in Angola was to support Jonas Savimbi, the charismatic leader of the right-wing, anticommunist guerrilla force, the National Union for the Total Independence of Angola (UNITA).

One of my responsibilities once I was in Europe was to cover the ruling Popular Movement for the Liberation of Angola (MPLA), which had been engaged in a brutal war with UNITA and the now much-weaker Angolan National Liberation Front (FNLA) since independence from Portugal in 1975.

This was probably the first time I found my reporting being challenged for political reasons. We received information from our penetrations of the Soviet-allied Angolans that contradicted what was coming from Kinshasa, which covered UNITA. We took a lot of flak for that from Washington. One senior official at the agency got very upset. When UNITA commandos blew up a gigantic concrete bridge over the Cuanavale River in eastern Angola as part of a vicious ongoing struggle for control of Cuito Cuanavale—a red line for Savimbi, whose headquarters were about 250 miles to the south—the blast didn't just knock out the bridge; it obliterated the pylons. It was a terrific success for the antigovernment forces, whose enemies consequently lost an important route for their tanks and artillery to reach the front line. The destruction was so complete that it had to have been done by professionals. Everyone was saying how well the Americans must have trained the rebels. But my sources in Europe and Africa were telling me it was the work of South African commandos disguised as UNITA forces. This was a sensitive subject, because the presidential authorization specifically banned cooperation with South Africa in the war. It was also hard psychologically for headquarters to hear because it suited their purposes to portray UNITA as an independent entity that fought its own battles. One of my critics accused me of being a racist because my reporting didn't fall in line with the myth. This was ridiculous. The implication was that I couldn't believe they had done it without white assistance. I was being disloyal to the program by believing our reporting, which showed that UNITA was in fact functioning as a corps of the South African army.

But my sources on the responsibility for the bridge attack were solid. I distinctly recall having a row with the chief of Africa about it. "Savimbi is an impressive guy," I said. "But he's not Thomas Jefferson." The chief lost it with me. "You're too young to be so goddamned cynical," he yelled. It was obvious to me that the prevailing view of Savimbi was myopic, to put it politely. We were allowing ideology to influence our actions and seeing the war through a political lens. The issue remained a constant strain throughout my time in Europe, where I managed the European end of the Angola program and kept an eye on Mozambique until I returned to Washington in August 1990.

The trouble was that the Republicans were inclined to see Savimbi as a great freedom fighter for democracy. In fact, he was more of a great freedom fighter for himself and his people, the

Ovambo ethnic group. In the end, after pouring hundreds of millions of dollars into a proxy war, it began to dawn on people that Savimbi was not quite what we thought, and that without our support he was doomed to failure. All we had done was supply him with enough hardware to defend himself—not enough to win the war.

We saw Angola as a front in the Cold War, when in fact it was a battle between ethnic groups and between northerners and southerners. Imposing our thinking on it, as we have in Iraq, led us to misunderstand the conflict. Having said that, there was a point in the early 1980s after Reagan came in when it looked like Savimbi might actually succeed because he was getting huge support, first from the South Africans, and then, increasingly, from us. We armed him well, but we never gave them enough heavy offensive equipment to defeat the MPLA.

The goal was supposed to be to drive the Cubans, East Germans, and Russians out of Africa and hand them a defeat. We achieved that goal, but they left before the fighting between UNITA and MPLA had been resolved. Still, UNITA managed to push back out of southern Angola, and even held elections in the region they controlled.

Then perestroika happened, and the Russians and the Cubans pulled out, like all colonialists do, in the middle of the night. The South Africans left later, when Namibia won independence in 1990. Our program petered out in the early 1990s after peace talks finally began. The fighting, needless to say, continued. After peace accords were signed in May 1991, a unity government was formed and Savimbi became minister of defense. The lull didn't last long. The situation deteriorated the following year in the run-up to September elections, which MPLA leader Jose Eduardo dos

Santos won. Savimbi refused to accept the results, which were declared fair by the UN and by us. There were unemployed, armed men roaming the country with nothing else to do but cause trouble. UNITA forces destroyed schools, hospitals, and dams. They targeted MPLA sympathizers. It all came to a head after the authorities cancelled a UNITA rally in Luanda on October 31. The government clamped down hard on UNITA, executing soldiers, officials, sympathizers, and civilians alike. Savimbi managed to escape; he returned to his base in the African bush, and the war resumed in earnest.

When Clinton came in, he decided a new direction was needed to end the fighting. This was the type of hard pragmatic choice that had to be made to resolve the seemingly endless conflict, but it was a hard one for me and some of the other veterans of the war to take. He declared the MPLA the legitimate government and said UNITA had to join it. But they resisted repeated cease-fire attempts.

The final sad twist came in 2002, when I got a call from the chief of Africa. "I just wanted to let you know," he said, "that we just got a report that the Gallo Negro [the black cockerel, Savimbi's nom de guerre] has been killed." Suddenly it became clear that Savimbi was UNITA and UNITA was Savimbi. All of the old Cold War rhetoric seemed pretty hollow. In the end, once the Cubans left, it was a war based on ancient tribal conflicts and personal relationships. Many of us had seen Savimbi's dynamic personality in action and knew that dos Santos was the prisoner of a corrupt puppet regime, and we were convinced that in time Savimbi would win. But the departure of the Soviets and their allies made dos Santos stronger as Savimbi became increasingly isolated. We were wrong about dos Santos, and it showed that first impressions are very unreliable in making policy decisions.

When I think about this war I always go back to what the former chief of Africa division, Dorwin Wilson, used to say in the early 1980s. Every big covert action has to have a clear beginning, middle, and end; otherwise the process takes on a bureaucratic and operational life of its own. The Angola program was always run with that in mind, but we had no Angolan strategy for success, which came so suddenly when the Soviet Union fell. It should have warned future administrations away from throwing themselves into interventions that might fail for lack of a convincing victory.

——

When I returned to the United States in July 1990, I was placed in charge of the central African region, a position that put me in the middle of an ongoing civil war in Chad and the beginning of the mess in Rwanda that culminated in the terrible genocide of 1994, in which machete-wielding murderers killed 800,000 men, women, and children in one hundred days. In both cases, the National Security Council under Bush senior failed to make the necessary policy changes resolutely and quickly enough to deal with the new, post-Cold War reality in the developing world.

Some of this was the result of the distraction with Iraq and the Gulf War, and, in fairness to the first Bush administration, they did try to build new alliances and enhance the role of the UN. But things moved slowly, and for the most part these African countries were left to settle our proxy wars as we, and the Soviets, pulled back. In a time that called for rapid policy innovation, we were left to deal with each crisis on a case-by-case basis. Disaster resulted.

The Clinton administration was blamed for failing to intervene in the Rwanda catastrophe. It suffered from a similar lack of direction at first in the Balkans, but eventually they were able to build on the efforts of the first Bush administration and establish new alliances. Unfortunately, in my view, much of this was lost, if temporarily, in the second Bush administration's build-up to the second Iraq war.

Clinton came in with a deep suspicion of the agency, but nonetheless seemed focused on how to revamp it for the post-Cold War era, a focus we shared in Europe. I had an incredible sense of déjà vu. We were certain the administration would hate the agency because they couldn't shake off their beliefs from the antiwar movement in the 1960s and '70s. But Clinton ended up being very supportive of us.

I was fortunate at that time to have an extremely dynamic boss in Milton Bearden, who was colorful and critical and larger than life, having witnessed the downfall of the Soviet empire as chief of the Soviet East European division. Milt's vision of building cooperative relationships on counterproliferation and counterterrorism based on mutual respect would guide many of my later decisions as chief of Europe.

We didn't exactly help the Clinton people in their search for a way to update the CIA with our failure to define a new role for ourselves. The sad thing is that the officers in our directorate, particularly in the field, realized that the agency's human intelligence function had always gone far beyond coverage of the Soviet Union, touching almost every area of interest to the U.S. government—political, economic, and military. Our instincts were to

avoid wide discussion of what we were about, and in the bureaucratic struggle for funds in the post-Cold War period, this killed
us. We had always seen ourselves as silent and stoic, but the real
world of the 1990s was much more complicated. We were slow
to define the terrorist target, but this was a reflection of the
problem that both the Clinton and second Bush administrations
had. Intelligence services react to the goals and prejudices of the
political leadership. It was particularly galling to hear people
who had no idea at all of facts hold forth as to how overt collection and émigrés could provide most of what was needed by the
government. At the end of the day we all paid for this debate,
which spanned both the Clinton administration and the second
Bush administration.

Without question, the most memorable event of my time in
Europe was the discovery that Aldrich Ames, a longtime officer of
the Soviet and Eastern Europe division, had been spying for the
Russians since at least 1985. I was sitting in Bearden's office when
he read the cable informing us that Ames had been arrested for
espionage. Clinton went on television to announce the development and described it as "serious." It was almost unprecedented
for a U.S. president to say anything so direct about the CIA in
public. We were thrown completely out of whack. In one European country alone, we had to abandon dozens of sources related
to a variety of issues because we believed they had been compromised by Ames, who had worked out how to access computer
databases across the agency. We're really in for it now, said Milt.
Any confidence the Clinton White House had in us was wrecked.

The execution of several of our sources in Russia was stunning,
and the reaction of the government reflected the emotions and
concerns involved. A number of senior officers were forced out,

and Bearden decided to retire. The Ames case has been covered in detail in a number of books and articles, and it is true that we needed to make changes in the wake of the Cold War, but I have always thought it was a mistake to say that Ames was the result of the culture in the Directorate of Operations. In fact, this was a classic espionage case, and we would be arrogant to think that our officers cannot be recruited by other services. This is why we maintain an aggressive counterespionage and security program for the entire service. After Ames, there was a period that lasted five or six years where we tried to reinvent ourselves in ways that addressed preconceptions from people outside the service. Tenet, in one of his most important acts, realized that it was a mistake to dilute the professional skills and traditions built up in the directorate. Instead, we needed to define our targets carefully and to make certain that our officers realized they had the support of management when they took operational risks. The appointment of the highly respected Jack Downing to run the directorate and Jim Pavitt as his deputy in 1997 signaled the end of the frenzy surrounding Ames. These developments allowed the counterintelligence experts to study the case quietly and carefully and to figure out how to guard against similar disasters in the future.

The last years of the 1990s were spent attempting to redefine our operations to address counterterrorism and proliferation, and in the ongoing fight for resources that ended on September 11. We also got bogged down contemplating what new techniques to adopt, trying to reinvent the wheel. There was a constant debate about whether to treat terrorism as a separate issue or whether to focus on geographical regions. The answer was staring us in the face: we needed to concentrate on all the issues, and because they overlap, you can address them region by region. Clinton headed in the right direction with his emphasis on the nexus between weapons proliferation and terrorism. But we were floundering around. As Bearden used to say, "We'd better figure this out or they're gonna padlock the place." In these years, we inched closer to our self-destruction.

Meanwhile, the budget cutbacks in Washington sent a message that we had to do more with less. That is partly why we ended up with the idea that there would be boutique areas of interest, where what we needed to do was start building our muscles for the war on terrorism. There was a focus on finding Osama bin Laden, yes, but not on finding sources for him in Europe, as we now know we desperately need to do. The prevailing wisdom was to pursue high-level targets and not waste time on the local communities. We now know that this was a mistake—fortunately one that has been corrected. Our human reporting is improving as we concentrate on doing what we know best, recruiting agents and building a comprehensive body of intelligence reporting. This is a time-consuming and difficult course, hardly surprising when you consider the life-changing commitment someone makes when they agree to spy for us. We have to be on guard to avoid taking seemingly more attractive and simpler paths, which lead away from the collection of real, clandestine intelligence.

For a spy–agent relationship to work, there has to be a shared sense of commitment to something, as well as explicit recognition of the risk involved, which, particularly in terrorist cases, can be death. Of course money helps, too, but it can't be the only incentive and is often a minor factor in a recruitment. It is particularly important to remember that one of the keys to recruiting someone is the belief that the United States represents a moral force for good in the world. But each agent is an individual, and there are no set rules of engagement. Rather, there are personal skills; skills that can only be learned through experience, by watching older officers carry out their operations. I fear that the politicization of the agency is leading to a deterioration of discipline and knowledge as officers are pushed out as punishment for mistakes made. More worryingly, the elevation of particular groups closer to the director's ear makes it harder for lower-level management to enforce the rules.

In 1995 my family returned to the United States, happy to have the Ames chapter behind us. I was put in charge of central group in Europe. Linda got a job at the Directorate of Intelligence (Linda had given up her full-time career when we went overseas and was forced to take whatever jobs were available during the periods we were in the States. Eventually, in 1996, she had enough of this cycle and left the agency and returned to college, where she eventually earned a masters degree and became a teacher of English as a second language). I was promoted to chief of operations for the European division the following year, and to deputy chief of Europe in July 1997, when I was also promoted to the senior service. Within a year, we found ourselves headed back to Europe, to what was then the biggest office overseas, in Europe. I was to experience one of the high points of my career in a spying coup that helped spark the Kosovo intervention.

There are moments in the modern world where, driven by pressing humanitarian or economic interests, democratic governments are going to be called upon to take action. Whatever the conspiracy theorists might say, Kosovo was one of those moments. Slobodan Milosevic was poised to exact widespread murder against the ethnic Albanian majority and someone had to stop him. I'm not saying Clinton got everything right. But on this score, he was right to intervene. At the time I thought we wasted weeks trying to decide whether to bomb or not. I wish we had wasted a bit more time before going to Iraq.

We had plentiful sources on the ground in Kosovo, some of which were our own, but many of which came through our allies. Our close relationships led us to the heart of Milosevic's plans for the Kosovar Albanians. Called "Operation Horseshoe," it basically involved sending in his troops in a horseshoe shape to capture and expel the Kosovar Albanians.

Our sources remained extremely productive and valuable throughout the war. We received information that Milosevic was planning to move surface-to-surface missiles into range of NATO camps in Bosnia. He backed off after the bombing began.

Madeleine Albright was very involved in our activities. We kept the State Department informed of operations we were planning, and most of the serious ones seemed to find their way to her desk eventually, as the memos would come back signed by her. Looking back, while at the time I did worry about her direct involvement in these working-level issues, I would have welcomed such intervention four years later, when we were involved in a debate with the analysts at WINPAC over Curveball. It's one thing to argue, as I do, that the president should not get involved in the day-to-day running of the agency. It is quite another when a highly sensitive operation is under way. Then the commander in chief should definitely be taking a—dispassionate—interest.

Reflecting on my European postings, I am reminded of the conversations I have had over the years with European counterparts who never tired of telling me how the United States had to understand that sometimes they couldn't be seen to agree with us for political reasons, but that didn't mean they didn't support us. Similarly, they always reminded me that Europeans often need us to take the lead in difficult interventions. I believe Iraq could have been done properly with support from more of our European allies had we handled them more sensitively. Kosovo is still a mess, but at least there is a truly international effort to keep it going in the right direction, and I'm sure it will succeed in the end. In Iraq, we still haven't figured out what direction we're going in.

It is frustrating to consider the way this administration has missed an opportunity to turn the CIA into a useful weapon. President Bush enjoyed immense goodwill at the agency when he was first elected, but I can say with some authority that that is no longer the case.

At first, there was a feeling that we'd be on top of the world. But gradually, we began to see the reappearance of some of the conservative ideologues of the Reagan administration—notably Elliott Abrams, who until recently served as the current president's special assistant for the Middle East, and Richard Perle, a chief ideologue of the Iraq War—who saw the agency as a hotbed of secret liberals. I never have figured out the source of this view, but after the 2000 election, it resurfaced. I warned my friends that, contrary to their rosy view of the new administration, we were likely to be in for a rough ride. Unfortunately, with the rise of Porter Goss, I would be proven right.

Chapter Nine

RULES OF THE ROAD

Langley, Virginia. Summer 2003

O ne day a member of the staff working for Porter Goss, a Florida Republican and chairman of the House Permanent Select Committee on Intelligence, who had served as a covert officer in the 1960s, told me he and his associates were planning for the day when their boss would replace Tenet and become director of central intelligence. Goss's staff had drawn up a list of people who would be pushed out because they were not deemed politically loyal. At that time, so this staffer told me, Pavitt and Kappes, two of the agency's most experienced officers, were on that list. I could not believe it. As part of a political game, he was planning to erase key holders of our institutional memory at a time when we needed desperately to refocus our abilities and dig deep into successful experiences of the past.

Unbeknownst to his colleagues, this staffer was also hedging his bets against the chance Goss would not replace Tenet by keeping me updated on the machinations in his camp. This was the aspect of being at headquarters that I liked least. As it turned out, the planned purge was just the tip of the iceberg. Later, Goss fulfilled his ambitions and replaced Tenet, becoming one of the most political directors ever to walk through the agency's doors. He nailed his colors to the mast shortly after Bush's reelection, accusing the upper echelons of the agency of harboring political affiliations none of us had. The *New York Times* and *Washington Post* gave prominent coverage to a November 2004 memo in which Goss reportedly laid out the "rules of the road" for his staff, saying they were to distance themselves from any and all criticism of the administration and its policies. Jaws dropped. It was as if he completely missed the point. We all knew it was our job to collect intelligence and not to stir the political pot. We found ourselves wondering if he knew what his job was supposed to be.

But at first, what perturbed me most about Goss was his staff's focus on settling personal scores.

As part of his duties as chairman, Goss and his staff regularly visited CIA stations. These visits began to stray from oversight of our activities, which was supposed to ensure we were following the law and using our funds wisely, into information-gathering exercises aimed at collecting negative comments from officers regarding management of the agency in general and the Directorate of Operations in particular. We were well aware of these efforts, but chalked them up to old disputes between some of Goss's staffers and members of the agency.

Some months later, Goss made a visit to Europe that would affect me personally. Throughout this period, he and his staffers were particularly interested in the continent. The volume and level of work there had increased substantially on my watch and there was a lot to talk about. However, this visit seemed to lead to me joining Pavitt and Kappes on the hit list. I've never been sure why. I suspect I made some personnel decisions that dragged me into the bureaucratic crossfire. In any event I suddenly found myself in the wrong camp for no good reason. It seemed irresponsible to me to be making such crucial personnel decisions on the basis of personal affiliations rather than ability and experience at one of the most challenging times in our history.

But when I first heard about the list, I dismissed the matter as a product of the staffer's overactive imagination. I told him it was a ridiculous notion, that the people being targeted were apolitical, like most of us at the agency. I was wrong to underestimate its importance.

I had met Goss, and I couldn't believe he would tolerate this foolishness by his staff, especially since I had always found him to be a supporter of the chain of command. In fact, he and I had always agreed that the agency command structure, while it needed to be streamlined, was important to the conduct of secure operations in the field. Now, after what transpired, I am not sure where he really stood. In the end, in a time of real crisis, my decision to ignore what I saw as bureaucratic intrigue—typical of Washington at its most irritating—would lead to my retirement.

As the months went on, it became clear that Goss would be the likely replacement for Tenet. We also began to hear more and more stories that the White House believed officers in the CIA were leaking information to damage the president's reelection campaign. I heard this from members of Goss's staff and from a well-connected ambassador in Europe, so the writing was on the wall. Linda and Livy remember those months as really tough and emotional, with many phone calls from my worried colleagues. I'd sometimes be up until 3 A.M. reassuring case officers in other time zones that I was not about to quit, even though I had mixed feelings at that point. Linda, meanwhile, was studying for her teaching exams and trying to stay focused on that, but she and I would spend hours rehashing what had gone on that day at work. Everyone in the service was walking on eggshells, scared they would not survive the purge that now did not seem so far-fetched. It was beneath the surface, but it was distressing all the same. A colleague of ours even declined an invitation to Linda's graduation party because he was worried about what the Goss guys would think. That just made us sad.

None of us stood up and said I quit, right there and then, not that I suppose anyone would have cared, though my old friend Pavitt was the first to talk about leaving. But Tenet stole his thunder.

— —

In early 2004, as the 9/11 commission began its very public work on who was to blame for the attacks, rumors began to swirl that both Tenet and Pavitt would retire.

I was called before the commission staff twice. Once it was to discuss the Hamburg cell. One of the staffers was, at first, inclined to blame us for that. But in the end, the panel chose to assign no blame, largely because we really had not had an opportunity to prevent the cell from forming.

The second time I spoke to the commission, it was to discuss the future of the CIA. I told them they were going in the right direction by trying to force information sharing between intelligence and law-enforcement services, which would cut down on the ability of individual analysts and agencies to feed reports straight to the Pentagon and White House without cross-checking with other agencies and sources. But I told them they were using the wrong approach. They had to make the agency and the entire intelligence community smaller and more efficient. It is particularly important that the focus of the operational portions of the intelligence community be on work in the field and not on their Washington structure. As they described their plans to me, it appeared that they were building another level of bureaucracy to deal with issues in Washington. Creating a structure to manage the fifteen entities that make up the community, as has been done, only perpetuates the problem. What we need is to reduce the number of agencies duplicating each other's work.

——

Pavitt had been assistant deputy director for operations and then deputy director for operations for a total of seven years, two as assistant deputy director and five as deputy director. None of his predecessors reaching back to 1980 had stayed at this level for more than two to three years total. He had been an executive assistant to several deputy directors for operations in the late 1980s and had served as intelligence coordinator at the NSC before returning to the agency to manage counterproliferation matters. He really cared about the officers in the covert branch, and wanted to improve their working conditions and benefits so we could compete with private industry for new officers. He worked hard to build morale, but he and Tenet never really had a chance to develop a long-term plan for operational direction. They were forced instead to deal with the post-Cold War budget debate, which focused on what level of money and personnel the agency needed in the modern world.

But some of the people around Goss despised Pavitt, and Tenet, for what they saw as personal and professional slights they felt they had suffered, for example during some of the more heated debates before 9/11 over resources. Every time I heard about one of these issues, it amazed me how angry these fellows were over incidents that seemed trivial at best. But when it became clear that the 9/11 commission would slam Pavitt personally, as it did Tenet, and that they were both to be blamed for every controversial policy decision on terrorism that they had been asked to carry out, it seemed inevitable they would both retire.

In late May 2004, the heads of European CIA bases met. Everyone was wondering who in their division would be out and who would be in. The theory in my circles was that Kappes would become deputy director for operations and Sulick would be the assistant deputy, with Mary Margaret Graham taking over the number-three job at counterintelligence. But it was all talk.

Tenet addressed the conference and, as usual, someone had to ask the inevitable question—how long would he stay? "I don't know," he said. "I've got to go. I have a meeting with the president at the White House."

The next morning we all learned he had turned in his retirement notice at that meeting. Tenet is a very private person and he kept this decision to himself. I found out the next morning from a British colleague who had heard the first announcement on television. I called Kappes and asked if it was true. Even he hadn't heard the news. The only person whom George had told apart from McLaughlin was Pavitt.

I ran into Tenet the next day in the hallway. "It wasn't because of the conference, was it?" I asked jokingly.

He called us all to the auditorium, or bubble, as we like to call it. People were crying. He was well liked. I didn't go down, though, as I can't stand mob scenes and I hoped to get a chance to talk to him quietly, without hundreds of people looking on. I felt we had a personal relationship. I watched his speech on the internal television channel and wondered to myself if they would pick Goss to replace him, and hoped they would not. My wish was that McLaughlin would stay on a while, at least until the election in November.

I came downstairs just as Tenet was leaving the bubble and walked straight into him. He was with his wife and son and seemed almost relieved, though melancholic. With tears in his eyes, he grabbed me in a huge bear hug. McLaughlin, who was taking over as acting director, was standing right behind him. "I'm going to need your help," he said. "You've got it, boss," I said. Tenet stayed on as director for about a month.

While Pavitt loved his job and didn't want to leave on a bad note, he did finally ask us all to congregate in the bubble a few days later, saying he had something important to announce about the future of the directorate. We all knew what was coming next. It seemed tragic. He had fought to win more funding from Congress, and in the rush to find someone to blame, the very people who had refused to grant him those funds were contributing to his demise. He had always said that between 1999 and 2000, the House intelligence committee, chaired by Goss since 1997, had refused to grant funds he had sought in order to hire hundreds of new officers and expand human intelligence operations. The rationale was that the Directorate of Operations was incapable of managing its budget, and the committee tried to use that argument to impose restrictions on funding. Their positions in these debates often reflected their personal, amateur prejudices regarding operational activity. They were trying to meddle in the day-to-day details of operations whereas their job was supposed to be oversight. Only after the September 11 attacks did we get all the cash we sought for "humint"—the human intelligence we were now told we so sorely lacked!

Pavitt wanted to do the right thing by his officers. He thought it was his job to improve morale. He was probably too decent a guy for the job. After I warned him about the list, instead of engaging in a major bureaucratic war that would have hurt the entire service, he chose to continue his real work. In the end he was too decent a person to take on these new political forces. I would miss him.

Everyone listened quietly to his speech, which lacked the drama of Tenet's because it had been so anticipated. He devoted most of it to praising people for their successes, and I was proud to hear him mention some of the operations we had carried out in Europe. Then he left.

I remember saying to Pavitt some time around then how I missed the clarity of the old days. It was true we had to reform, but the government needed to learn from its mistakes, too. I thought about my family, and all the sacrifices they had made when we were abroad. We had so much experience to pass on from those years. Back then, we took risks, sacrificed lives, and honed our skills for a greater good we could all understand. Now, it was as if our knowledge was being tossed aside for political reasons, as if a destructive purge at headquarters would make the White House look better. From a personal perspective, it seemed so unfair, after all the risks we had taken in Africa and in Europe, after all those years in the shadows in service to our country. But on a far more important professional note, we had something to tell the next generation. It seemed like a terrible waste that some of the most experienced people of my generation were going to be denied that opportunity.

Chapter Ten

THE NEW BOYS

Langley, Virginia. July 2004

During my last few months at headquarters, a rash of stories popped up in the press about a war between the White House and the CIA. They were true, broadly speaking, but it was not a war of our making. The White House and conservative commentators became hyperparanoid that we were trying to undermine Bush with negative assessments of the situation in Iraq, a response that would not have been entirely surprising considering how badly the administration had compromised us. It was an odd reminder of the end of the Carter administration, when Casey, in his role as Reagan campaign manager, was suspected of trying to delay the release of the hostages in Iran until after the elections (though a congressional investigation found no evidence for such a conspiracy).

In our case, the charges were simply false. McLaughlin himself hinted at the true picture when he wrote in the *Washington Post* that CIA officers saw it as their "solemn duty" to work for the president "regardless of which party holds the White House." We had just called it as we saw it, he wrote, and it had been advantageous to people with a "wide array of motives" to put this material out when the CIA's views seemed at odds with the administration's. John is a very honorable, professional officer, and I believe he found these accusations distasteful at best. To ascribe evil motives to officers who had taken great risks for their country and government over the years was an outrageous political gambit, which was, if anything, symbolic of the destructive political environment. There were plenty of leaks during the campaign, from throughout the government, but they didn't come out of the leadership of our directorate. In fact, the administration would do well to look to its own house when discussing the strategic use of leaked information.

It became clear that summer that Goss was the likely candidate to fill Tenet's shoes. It would be a bitter pill to swallow. Aside from everything else, Goss, clearly with his own agenda in mind, had been stirring up criticism from his position as chairman of the House intelligence committee that June, describing our branch as a "stilted bureaucracy incapable of even the slightest bit of success." By their very definition, our successes cannot be advertised because they are secret, so it seemed like a low blow.

In mid-July, before they left, Tenet and Pavitt had picked Kappes to replace Pavitt, and made Sulick his most senior deputy. These choices were a great morale boost. Behind the scenes, according to published media reports, Kappes had pulled off an incredible disarmament coup in the Middle East, persuading Muammar Gadhafi to give up his weapons of mass destruction. Kappes had survived the 9/11 report, retaining the support of both sides of the aisle, and as a former CIA office chief, he was exactly the kind of guy we needed to shape the future. Sulick, meanwhile, a decent, tough, strong-minded fellow, had done important work in the Balkans and had run a major office, and his promotion was widely welcomed. These two men were perfectly matched in their positions. Kappes is extremely disciplined, a former commander of the fabled Silent Drill Platoon in the Marines, whose exhibitions of unparalleled precision, in their gleaming blue-and-white dress uniforms and fixed bayonets, are the envy of the armed services. He is the archetypal manager, a born leader. Sulick is the character of the pair, tough and quirky and brimming with inspiration and sharp instincts. They were a powerful combination. It was ironic that Kappes was on the Goss hit list, since he had been responsible for delivering the most tangible disarmament success story in Bush's presidency.

As for myself, I was happy to stay in charge of Europe and get a grip on the terrorist threat there. I was highly driven by that goal. It was a challenge we were already addressing, one that could bring measurable successes. Also, it seemed to me that Goss would come in and my colleagues would have it tougher than they realized. I thought—foolishly, perhaps—that I'd be able to help them navigate treacherous waters.

Bush nominated Goss in August and received mixed responses for his decision. Whether or not Goss was right for the job, I think it was a mistake to nominate a replacement for Tenet before the elections. That single decision confirmed my impression more than anything that had come before that the intelligence gathering in this administration was politicized as never before. It was hard not to question the timing, just a few weeks before the reelection campaign, when Bush's National Guard record was at issue and Kerry was being depicted as a coward despite having served valiantly in Vietnam. It seemed to some observers that this most politically savvy of administrations could not have failed to choose Goss, an eight-term congressman who had criticized Kerry, with the election in mind. It was equally hard not to conclude that he was being picked to silence dissenters at the CIA.

If any one lesson was to be drawn from the 9/11 report, which recommended creating the new post of national intelligence director and shaking up the CIA's analytical and spying operations, it was that politics had to be set aside as much as possible when it came to intelligence gathering. How else could the problems that the September 11 bloodbath exposed be fixed? Goss could hardly be described as apolitical, and in that sense he was an unwelcome choice at an agency that sees itself first and foremost as duty-bound. Goss had been in Congress for many years, and as Democrats cheerfully reminded everyone shortly after his nomination, had in the late 1990s cosponsored legislation that would have cut human intelligence staff by one fifth. This was an uncomfortable fact for the Bush administration, which had been slamming Kerry for proposing cuts in the intelligence budget at the same time that were smaller than those considered by Goss— except, of course, for the CIA.

The tussle between the White House and the CIA started to

turn into a full-blown political horror show later that year. Bush, during a visit to the United Nations in September at which he made no apologies for going to war to disarm a country of weapons it did not have, turned his guns on the CIA. It was impossible to know whether he was being naive or deeply cynical when he offered the following analysis of a new National Intelligence Estimate, which had offered a gloomy outlook of the situation in Iraq. In it, he said, "The CIA laid out several scenarios. It said that life could be lousy, life could be OK, life could be better. And they were just guessing as to what the conditions might be like. The Iraqi citizens are defying the pessimistic predictions." (Later he said he should have said "estimate," not "guess.")

It was rich, coming from the leader of an administration that had used a faulty National Intelligence Estimate the year before to go to war.

The leak to the *New York Times* of details in the estimate, prepared in July, preceded Bush's trip to New York with the interim leader of Iraq, Iyad Allawi, by just a few days. It was bad timing for Bush. He evidently assumed that the leak was designed to hurt his election chances. Yet all the estimate did was state the inevitable conclusion that Iraq faced one of three possible scenarios—a tenuous stability, political fragmentation, or civil war. Speaking the truth, as it turned out, was less popular with the administration than offering up shaky sources touting "evidence" that Saddam had weapons of mass destruction.

Paul Pillar, one of the report's authors and the national intelligence officer for the Near East and South Asia, discussed the estimate at a dinner in San Francisco and was blasted by conservative columnist Robert Novak (who, coincidentally, was also the first journalist to report Plame's identity). According to Novak, Pillar also said the CIA had concluded early in the administration that military intervention in Iraq would intensify anti-American hostility in the Muslim world. Pillar denied being the source of the leak to the *New York Times*, but Novak concluded that the CIA wanted a "license to criticize the president" and Tenet. This was just not true.

Things became downright ridiculous in the first week of October when the press got their hands on a story about Michael Kostiw, chosen by Goss to replace Buzzy Krongard after he resigned as executive director, the number-three position in the agency, and returned to the private sector. Kostiw had been caught shoplifting a $2.13 packet of bacon from a supermarket in Langley in 1981, when he had been a case officer for ten years, the *Washington Post* reported. This meant that he had had to resign and agree to seek counseling in order to avoid facing misdemeanor charges. Within days, Kostiw was forced to withdraw from consideration for the position in an embarrassment for Goss, who used his discretionary authority to appoint him instead as a senior adviser. But the story, leaked according to the *Post* by former CIA officials, took Kostiw out of the running for a position that would have put him in charge of dealing with disciplinary problems. Goss's staff, meanwhile, blamed my friends Sulick and Kappes for the leaks, but I would stake my life on it that they were not responsible. I said as much to the staffer who had drafted a report for Goss in June that accused us of being unable to reform and of micromanaging field resources. He was also one of the four members of the committee staff Goss brought with him, but only after creating the post of special assistant for operations and analysis so he could fill it. (He also told me he and his colleagues liked to refer to themselves as "the revolutionaries." But one of my staff coined a less complimentary term for them that seems to have stuck, given the number of times I have seen it used in the media: "the Gosslings.")

The Goss people apparently did not believe me about the leaks. They increasingly considered me liberal and disloyal, I was told by friends. Though it was never communicated to me that I should go, as word spread that there would be more changes coming, I came to believe that I was on the list after all.

The worst of it was that Sulick and Kappes, a pair of former Marines and Cold War veterans who could hardly be accused of being Democrats in disguise, were so clearly in the line of fire. It didn't matter that they worked hard, that they had a plan to improve human intelligence gathering. The agency was in chaos. The trips to Europe by Goss and his entourage in their role as congressional overseers of the intelligence community had affected me, too. Some people apparently complained that I had pushed them too hard to change course and expand reporting on terrorist targets in Europe. That was enough to put me on the blacklist after decades of service that they could not possibly have appreciated.

As I've mentioned, I had nothing against Goss, who had always been amiable and a concerned listener, but the people he surrounded himself with seemed focused on unearthing any sign of disenchantment with us. They criticized us, saying we had been too risk averse. This was not true. Tenet and Pavitt had fought to remove restrictions put on operations during the administration of Deutch. Under Tenet, the number of operations and the quality of reporting improved dramatically.

I thought it was a great shame that Tenet resigned when he did. Had he stayed on until the election, he could have allowed for a smooth transition for Kappes and precluded many of the problems that followed. Even if Goss had then replaced Tenet, Kappes would have been well in place and things could have moved forward without the Machiavellian intrigue that served only to weaken the clandestine service. By inflating the problems and ignoring the very good work being done, these fellows created a whole series of unnecessary bureaucratic exercises. For instance, the directorate was forced to draw up its third five-year plan in four years—when things were already moving forward.

I want to give Goss's entourage the benefit of the doubt and believe they really wanted to make changes, some of which were needed. However, their methods and their lack of understanding of the intricacies of intelligence collection complicated this process—hopelessly so. They appeared to be listening to officers who had grown irritated by the demands that had been placed on them since the September 11 attacks to provide real sources. In my case, they were bothered by some of my personnel assignments as I tried to bring in senior officers with counterterrorist experience as opposed to traditional old European hands. These appointments had heralded a dramatic increase in reporting and more productive cooperation with our allies. I believe in the end that the Goss staffers and I were actually headed in the same direction, strategically speaking, and they might have discovered that if we had ever had a proper conversation.

By the fall, as I tried to give the new leadership an overview of European operations, I realized there was no hope. Ironically, the one man who seemed to get the point was Kostiw. He told me not to worry and that he would explain my thinking to them. By then, though, I had pretty well decided that I didn't have four years to waste while these guys figured out how things worked.

In the week before the 2004 election, my source in the Goss camp came to me and said that if Bush lost he would need me to help him find a job overseas. For over a year this fellow had been telling me of meetings the Goss staffers were having and of contacts with some disgruntled officers, as well as plans to draw up a list of senior officers who would be fired when Goss came into office. I passed these warnings on to Pavitt and Kappes, but always with the caveat that they sounded like the usual dramatic hyperbole you hear on a regular basis in a large organization made up of talented but eccentric individuals. In the end I realized that I had been wrong not to warn them more sternly about the threat to them, and to understand the seriousness of the fact that I, too, was on the list.

Looking back, though, I wouldn't have done anything differently. My job was to conduct clandestine operations, not engage in bureaucratic infighting with people who were much better at it than I was.

Chapter Eleven

FOUR MORE YEARS

Vienna, Virginia. November 2, 2004

L inda was running around counting her chickens before
they were hatched the night of the election, convinced
Kerry had won. From inside the house, where Livy and
I were watching the results creep in, we heard her sound the car
horn in a premature, celebratory blast as she returned from the
polls. She was so motivated by the way the Iraq War had begun
that she had become involved in campaign politics as never
before. She had captained the Democratic effort at our local
precinct to take Virginia back for the Democrats. It was around 9
P.M., and while our district had gone for a Democrat for the first
time in history, Virginia had just been called for Bush and what

had looked like Kerry's night was rapidly becoming the president's. Livy and I had already realized that the incumbent was going to win and be around for another four years—with potentially huge implications for our lives.

But Linda, who had broken out in shingles while campaigning for Kerry, was certain that a Democrat victory in her conservative precinct meant Kerry must have won. It had been one of the most divisive election campaigns ever and we felt personally affected by the mudslinging. It was the same for many of our friends. We knew one CIA couple in particular who were torn apart by the campaign. She was determined that Bush would win because of her views on abortion, even though it would almost certainly mean her husband, who was supporting Kerry, would lose his job—which he did.

Linda knew instantly that she had been wrong when she rushed into the house and saw the looks on our faces. She was crushed, and Livy was so mad that she went to school the next day and aced her Asian studies midterm exam. As for me, I braced myself.

Matters deteriorated quickly, and details of how Goss's staff tried to circumvent the covert branch's management and deal with the stations directly ended up being carried in detail in the press. This only fueled their belief that my directorate had leaked the information on Kostiw. They started to threaten senior officers, leading to a confrontation that, in turn, led to both Kappes and Sulick retiring.

It all started with a cable. Goss's people had contacted European stations directly about various matters, without going through the directorate management or the European office. It was nothing terrifically sensitive. It referred to seemingly mundane things such as travel plans by Goss, but the implication was that the management at headquarters was being sidelined. When my colleagues complained—I was on a trip myself at the time—they got their knuckles rapped.

A book by my colleague Michael Scheuer, *Imperial Hubris*, which had gone on sale that July and said we were losing the war on terrorism, only added to the negative perceptions of agency management, since CIA officers were responsible for vetting and approving the text. However, CIA officers have to follow strict rules when approving books by their colleagues. They can only remove text that reveals ongoing operations or sources and methods. They cannot remove opinions, however much they might disagree with them, so leaving in criticism of the administration certainly did not amount to an act of treason.

There was more baggage, frankly, on Goss's side. The negative impression of him grew further when he sent out a memo to the whole staff a few days after the election instructing us to "support the administration and its policies."

The departure of Kappes and Sulick happened suddenly, two weeks after the election. Basically, Kappes quit after he refused to sack Sulick for criticizing Pat Murray, Goss's chief of staff, at a meeting. McLaughlin and Buzzy left around the same time.

The showdown began three days after the election, on November 5. The Goss staffers had created an adversarial relationship with the office of the deputy director for operations. It led to a series of confrontations, particularly between Sulick and Murray, who had been Goss's staff director in Congress and had previously worked at the Department of Justice. Goss was involved in some of these meetings, though he did nothing to moderate the behavior of his staffers. In the end the hostilities led to a heated verbal exchange. Murray had sent Sulick a truly obnoxious e-mail in response to a memo he had written proposing an outreach program to Congress. I have since read the e-mail, and it was one of the rudest I've ever seen. It accused Sulick and Kappes, two of the most experienced, respected men in the building, of being fools and lacking integrity. At a meeting where Kappes and Sulick raised the congressional outreach initiative with Goss in Murray's presence, Murray claimed he did not have a copy of the e-mail handy and Sulick shoved a copy across the table to him. After Goss left his office for another meeting, Sulick confronted Murray and told him the Directorate of Operations would not tolerate being treated like a bunch of "Democrat congressional staffer 'pukes.'" They had managed to maintain a decent relationship before that, but now it was all over.

After the meeting, Murray asked Kappes to move Sulick to another job, but he refused. They took a weekend to think about it and came back to work on the Monday and told Goss they would both be resigning. I believe that the Goss staffers thought that Kappes would go along with them to keep his job. They misread the man; Kappes is that rare character in Washington, someone so honest he will not compromise his principles for anyone to keep a job. I spoke to him on several occasions after this incident, and he, in his straightforward way, had moved on and was not dwelling on this sad chapter in the history of the agency.

I remember Mike recalling how he had heard someone say that Murray had been born in 1968, the year he had arrived in Vietnam as a Marine rifleman. Recognizing this dissonance was enough to make Sulick realize he was probably going to have to go. For some at the CIA, the likes of Murray are just politicos, with no military or intelligence experience.

It was around then that the reports about the "rules of the road" memo surfaced. It rubbed a lot of people the wrong way in an agency that prides itself on not taking political sides but does not take kindly to being abused by its political masters. Not only were we to support the administration and its policies in our work, we were not to "identify with, support, or champion opposition to the administration or its policies." At the same time, we were to "provide the intelligence as we see it—and let the facts alone speak to the policy maker." I almost fell off my chair laughing. That's exactly what we had done, or tried to do, on Curveball, and look where it got us.

For me, the political shenanigans were getting to be too much. The distractions were extremely unwelcome. I was responsible for dozens of stations and many hundreds of people, most of them overseas. At night I was coming home more stressed out than ever. Livy and Linda again encouraged me to retire. You don't get paid enough, my daughter would say. Linda was terrified I would have a heart attack. I was in a real dilemma, not wanting to abandon my colleagues. I had always considered myself a team player, but as many of the people I knew and respected left, my isolation grew.

——

With the removal of Sulick and Kappes, the CIA lost two of its best officers, men who were in a position to lead change. The attacks on them and others were just a case of making changes to show that change was taking place. Part of the reason for this was that there was no one on the 9/11 commission, which recommended many of the changes now taking place in the community, with substantial intelligence experience. It was just like after Ames.

As I mentioned, the line the Goss people took with me was that I was a micromanager. I actually erred on the side of the station rather than headquarters, but I was determined to enforce good practice on source validation to avoid the kind of disaster that had happened with Curveball. But my approach created a pretext for them to question me. I don't take it personally. But I do think their trips abroad before Goss came in, when they would try to elicit negative comments from junior officers—or from me about Tenet and Pavitt—were damaging. In my case, their interventions undermined my efforts to demand quality sources, not some random guys who might or might not have useful information to share.

For all that, Goss seemed like the nicest guy in the world. Everyone says so. I have never had anything but the best conversations with him. He is, in every sense of the word, a politician. I disapproved of the way he refused to intervene in the battle between his staff, particularly Murray, and the Directorate of Operations management. One of his staffers actually told me that Goss stayed out of these affairs by design. "I don't deal with personnel matters," he said. "My staff does."

When Sulick and Kappes left, one of the other division chiefs called me. I was one of the most senior of the chiefs by then. I'd known him a long time—since college. "What are you going to do?" he said. "I don't want to leave right now," I answered. "I'm not really prepared to. But if I'm still on their blacklist by next summer as a Tenet and Pavitt loyalist, and I'm continuing to hear that Europe needs to be more aggressive when in fact we are doing more work than we've ever done, then I'm gone."

In the end I stayed in office only until the first of the year. It was clear that I would not be able to continue to pursue operations in Europe without interference, despite the fact that our field stations continued to do some of the best work ever carried out in Europe, achieving a number of historic firsts. At the same time our work with our European allies was moving in exciting new directions, and I was happy to see they chose one of the people I had recommended as my replacement. I believe he will continue to press for creative new ideas in addressing operations in Europe, particularly against the terrorist target.

When I asked for my retirement figures, word spread throughout the directorate and I began to be bombarded by e-mails asking about my future. At this point I felt I had to make a decision to ensure that my fate didn't become yet another distraction for the operations in the field.

I called Jose, who had been appointed deputy director for operations, and asked for a meeting. We talked briefly. Jose is an old friend and a good man and I believe he will do an excellent job— if the director's staff gives him room to operate. I had already had a long talk with him and he knew why I had come. I told him that my leaving had nothing to do with him and wished him well. He was gracious, and after a short discussion I left.

It was strange to walk down the seventh-floor corridor and realize that my career there was over. But it dawned on me that as my close friend, the chief of East Asia, would have said, after twenty-five years in the agency and thirty-one in the government, it was time to do something else.

I didn't have four more years to wait until these guys were gone.

Chapter Twelve

FAREWELL TO LANGLEY

Langley, Virginia. February 3, 2005

The day I turned in my badge at CIA headquarters, I signed a statement for the inspector general on a controversial terrorist case, visited the one close friend who had survived the arrival of Goss, and walked to the third-floor stairwell where I had proposed to Linda all those years ago. Then I went to the library for one last look around. As a young officer, I used to hide out there when I was exhausted. In recent years, it had become the place I would go when I was frustrated. But all that was behind me now.

I was walking past the directors' portraits when I ran into Jose's secretary, who said Jose wanted to see me to say a final good-bye. I thought for a second and decided that the time had come just to go. So I told her to tell Jose that I wished him all the best and that I had sent him one last, long e-mail earlier in the day. I had simply run out of things to say. And frankly, I had an ulterior motive; I didn't want to spoil my nostalgic melancholy by running into one or more of the other new inhabitants of the seventh floor.

In the note, I wrote that my only regret was that I wouldn't be there to help him. But you'll be better off, I wrote, because I'll only get you into trouble when you have to defend me from accusations I am a member of some liberal plot trying to undercut the president.

I made my way to the exit and handed my badge to the guard. "I wish I could retire too," she laughed. For a minute, I remembered the excitement of my first day at headquarters. Then I decided it was time to go home and forget all the soap opera.

The last person I saw was Cofer Black, who was leaving on the same day to start his new job in private industry after being seconded to the State Department for two years. We had a laugh about the Africa years, shook hands, and then I drove home. Linda and I spent the evening with the Sulicks as well as our friend who was chief of East Asia and his wife.

Many CIA marriages don't make it. Ours did because we formed a tight circle and, to some extent, retreated into ourselves. We became a little unit of defiance, all three of us. Linda and Livy are like that to this day, and I suppose my departure displayed the same tendency.

The situation was tough on Linda. After all her years at the agency, it's a shame they didn't try to harness her desire to get more involved. She would have liked to work in personnel, having experienced the difficulties of going abroad for the agency. She would have done a great job. But the agency has never really managed to figure out how to assist women in furthering their careers, far less spouses. Minorities have a hard time, too, as you might expect. There's no question that the CIA has to shake off its old boys' network image, and I did my best to help things along the way by promoting people who didn't sound and look like me. We should be smart enough to balance the need for change and the importance of experience and tradition, but all too often this balance eluded us.

Linda and Livy feel angry that there has been so little response here at home to the harsh truths about the Iraq War. It pains Livy in particular to see how little attention seems to have been paid to the rights and wrongs of it. Livy took part in protests when right-winger Joerg Haider was elected in Austria, and, without wishing to draw any comparisons, is always saying how she can't understand why there weren't more street protests here when Bush was reelected. She calls it a "new intellectual isolationism." I call it misinformation.

She was happy to see the Dearlove memo make it into the news. But to all of us, it seems the impact was rather short-lived. Livy says the administration felt obliged to rattle its sabers after 9/11, and someone had to be the scapegoat.

In those last months, when I would complain, Linda would remind me of my old mantra: "I love my job." "But I thought you loved your job," she would say, trying to get me to lighten up. It's been a draining time. Our extended families are still at odds over the election, and I feel like we've just emerged from a long, dark tunnel.

Coming out of the CIA cocoon to tell this story has been hard, too. For years, I have lived on the other side of a one-way mirror, among friends and beside enemies, never able to say who I really am. Linda still cannot tell most people I worked for the CIA. She has a close girlfriend she has known since she worked at the bank and she only told her after I retired. Her liberal Democrat friends don't understand. She thinks they probably see me as an agent of evil influence.

We had it drummed into us for so long: don't wave any red flags, don't talk about this or that, don't stand out. So you grow distant from your wider family and friends and grow closer to your agency friends. That's what made the way this war was begun and prosecuted so hard to take, because it often set us against each other.

I agree with many of the things Goss wanted to do, particularly his emphasis on pushing people into the field. In recent years many people in Washington have forgotten the difference between an intelligence organization based largely on briefing policy makers and a true espionage service focused on recruiting sources and producing secret intelligence. You need both functions, and ideally they should complement each other, but the balance has shifted toward the Washington side.

I had always believed in the CIA tradition of having analysis and operations in the same organization. But the events leading up to the Iraq War have convinced me that we need to draw clear lines between the functional areas of the intelligence community. The 9/11 commission and the Silberman-Robb panel that examined intelligence failures for the president were correct. All the analytical elements need to be grouped together to make certain nothing slips between the cracks. It is even more important for all of the operational, clandestine elements to be pulled together into a separate, truly clandestine service under the new director of national intelligence (DNI), John Negroponte. That way he will have a flat structure to manage, with direct control over separate elements for analysis—including counterterrorism—and operations, technical matters, and administration. This can only happen if he has full control not only at the CIA, but also at the Department of Defense, the FBI, and the other services scattered across the U.S. government. Because the CIA and the intelligence community as a whole are middle-aged organizations, this will require radical change, particularly vis-à-vis the authorities of the secretary of defense and other powerful officials. But it is the only way we can guarantee an effective espionage service, free of political influence. The DNI structure provides the perfect vehicle for this change, but not as it is currently drawn up. Rather than try to find a way to coordinate and accommodate all the disparate parts of the intelligence community, the DNI needs to establish direct control of the whole community and make it clear that we don't need fifteen services, but rather one effective organization.

Some of my old colleagues believe we are watching the death throes of the original CIA, and this may be true, but I still hold out hope that Negroponte can break down resistance within the Department of Defense and the FBI and unite the intelligence community in a way that will give the American people their money's worth.

One argument that will have to be overcome is the claim that having central control will weaken military tactical intelligence. That can be solved simply. Special forces and other tactical military intelligence units should remain under the control of military leaders. The DNI should only have direct control over traditional clandestine intelligence collection. In fact, one of the main problems we have in Iraq is that civilian CIA officers are tied up carrying out tactical collection operations that would be better done by Special Forces anyway.

The DNI will, of course, have to maintain the CIA paramilitary capability to address those tactical issues that for political or diplomatic reasons cannot be taken on by the military. But this is a very specialized function that should only be used when more appropriate military solutions are not available.

One development in mid-2005 suggested to me that it will be an uphill battle to introduce the necessary reforms. Duncan Hunter, the California Republican, insisted that Peter Hoekstra, the Michigan representative who took over Goss's chairmanship of the intelligence committee, include language in the 2006 budget that would have stopped Negroponte from transferring employees from agency to agency without asking congressional committees for approval first. This was a preposterous idea and it held up the approval process. Hunter only backed down after Negroponte personally promised to consult him before transferring any staff. This kind of attitude defeats the whole purpose of the reforms, which were supposed to make it easier to get our jobs done and simplify lines of command. No one argues with the need for military commanders in the field to control tactical intelligence units and assets, but it is important that traditional "humint" collectors in the Department of Defense work under the DNI with no ambiguity about who is in charge.

Fortunately, there is plenty of debate over the future structure of the agency and U.S. intelligence, although the nature of the discourse is sometimes frustrating. After I retired, I twice appeared before the commission chaired by Charles Robb, the former Virginia governor and senator, and Laurence Silberman, a senior circuit judge on the D.C. court of appeals, appointed by Reagan, and a former ambassador to Yugoslavia. I was questioned at length about Bill's tour around the world in pursuit of the Iraqi source, and I hoped the issue would be given a serious airing in the six-hundred-page report when it was released on March 31, 2005. But the only references I can find are oblique and seem designed to head off any criticism of the administration for failing to consider the possibility that Saddam was not armed to the teeth. This is no doubt a consequence of the fact that the panel, for all its eminence, excluded from its considerations the behavior of the administration, as it submitted its report to the president. But the decision to exclude the details of the story of how we tried to get to the Iraqi source still bothers me, especially when you remember that it is our most important job to find sources who give us timely intelligence in times of crisis. The report criticized us for our lack of quality human sources and noted the "highly compartmented" nature of Saddam's regime. It was unclear, the panel concluded, whether "even a source at the highest levels of the Iraqi government would have been able to provide true insight into Saddam's decision-making." The Iraq case, the report says, suggests "inherent limitations" of human intelligence collection. That's quite right, but the entire point of our craft is to collect intelligence from people. So are we to conclude, then, that there was no point in talking to this senior Iraqi because we couldn't be sure if he was lying? The point they missed—because it was outside the scope of their study—was that the decision makers only wanted to hear the intelligence that suited them. In such an environment, the likes of Curveball and the Niger documents achieved a credibility they never deserved.

I could scarcely agree more with Silberman-Robb's conclusion that failing to conclude Saddam had ended his weapons programs was one thing, and failing even to consider it as a possibility was quite another, especially since we absolutely did consider it, but the president was only interested in using our source as a prop in his case for war.

I agree, too, as they say in the report—quoting Charles Duelfer, who took over the CIA-run Iraq Survey Group from David Kay in its search for weapons in Iraq—that it is unlikely that more than a handful of people knew about Saddam's decision to halt his weapons programs, and that a human source in Saddam's inner circle might not have been enough to see the truth. But getting to this individual would have allowed us to come a step closer and perhaps have opened our eyes.

The other pertinent observation made by Silberman-Robb is that liaison services can gain us access to sources we could not otherwise reach. The would-be Iraqi source is the perfect example of this. But since he was talking to such a publicly critical ally on the Iraq War, the policy makers clung to their prejudices and decided not to bother hearing what the Iraqi had to say. It may be true, as the report says, that not a single analytical product was generated over the course of twelve years that examined the possibility that Saddam had destroyed his weapons. But President Bush heard directly about our attempts to talk to the Iraqi, who knew the weapons programs were virtually nonexistent, and our leader was clearly not interested in pursuing him; otherwise Bill would have been stuck in coach class considerably longer than he was.

If Negroponte succeeds in his efforts, it will be up to the U.S. government to define the threats and goals in the war on terrorism, and in Iraq, more clearly. This is, of course, not as easy as it sounds. But our grand declarations about killing or capturing terrorists and defeating terrorism are meaningless unless we define who the terrorists are, what they want, and who supports them. We will have to take the excruciating step of facing the role we share with other Western states in the growth of corrupt, dictatorial governments in the Middle East. This is a legacy of both colonialism and the Cold War, when, to deal with the global threat posed by the Soviet Union, we often made a deal with the devil to gain the support of a dictator or corrupt group of rulers. This was a pragmatic, necessary policy, but we have to clean up the fallout. For many people in the Middle East, the West's historical role in the corruption of these governments is the living testament to their colonial pasts. Their isolation in émigré communities in Europe makes them susceptible to calls from radical leaders to join the struggle against Western culture. These leaders often play a double game, using the struggle to enhance their status in the community and in some cases enrich themselves. If we do not face up to that, we will never be able to change the paradigm and define the real nature of the terrorist threat we face today. The poor and disenfranchised of the region are drawn to Al Qaeda and other radical organizations that offer simple explanations for their plight, and a ready villain: the U.S. government and its allies. The only other possible explanation for the anger that we face there is that Arabs are evil. I don't buy that.

——

There is an interesting parallel in the 1960s and 1970s, when the West in general and Europe in particular faced an ongoing threat from violent, well-organized terrorist groups who assassinated political, military, and economic leaders across the continent. While the police and security services took serious, often draconian measures against terrorist groups like the IRA, Brigada Rosa, and the Red Brigades, they avoided making changes that altered the day-to-day lives of average Europeans. They felt that would have helped the terrorists achieve one of their main goals. They were tough, even violent, but they were careful not to curtail basic freedoms. I believe in the idea of a strong central government, but the sprawling bureaucracy that has been created at the Department of Homeland Security makes it difficult to address the terrorist threat in real terms. By the same token, Congress needs to look very carefully at the Patriot Act, much of which is very useful in counterterrorist operations, while other sections allow government intrusion into our private lives with no tangible operational return. At the same time, without clear, direct authority over the community, the office of the director of national intelligence risks becoming just another giant monster designed to satisfy political needs and to feed Washington's massive briefing machine.

In the field, what we need are intelligence professionals who really know what they're talking about, and not just people to fill slots. A friend of mine always likes to tell a story about a breathless cable a defense attaché once wrote saying the Afghan embassy had put black crepe over its doors and windows in a display of mourning for the September 11 dead. What he didn't recognize was that that was the mission of the royalist embassy of the former king, not the Taliban government. Another favorite is the officer who once reported travel by an all-black rugby team to apartheid-era South Africa as a sign of progress. It was, needless to say, the New Zealand All Blacks, a team named for the color of their shirts, not their skin. This is what happens when you have too many intelligence agencies.

At the end of my testimony to Silberman-Robb, Senator John McCain asked about morale at the agency. I told him that while there were problems at headquarters, at the end of the day, the officers in the field, the heart of the Directorate of Operations, drew their morale from the work. They deserved a well-organized management structure in Washington, where less is more.

As I contemplate the situation we face now, it seems to me that the real legacy of Aldrich Ames is the direct involvement of politicians and oversight personnel in the operational process. Instead of making certain that we are not breaking the law, they have become active players, second-guessing both how operations are carried out as well as personnel decisions. Under the Bush administration, this problem crept right up to the Oval Office, with the president directly involved in ways he should not have been in the day-to-day running of the intelligence community.

The fact is that intelligence work is not difficult, but politicians have to provide specific topics or requirements for coverage, and then not attempt to shape the answers we find in advance. We don't need more magical bureaucratic fixes. We need to devote ourselves single-mindedly to recruiting agents in Islamic communities around the world so that we can really see what's going on when the few individuals among them who seek to do harm start on a path of violence.

CIA case officers are an eccentric bunch; they are not exactly easy to manage, and if they were, they probably wouldn't be such good field officers. That is why the command structure should be as simple, and short, as possible. Everyone wants to be his or her own boss. The CIA needs oversight, but the way that process is run now is a disaster, with dozens of committees and subcommittees in Congress jealously guarding their piece of the oversight pie and fifteen intelligence agencies in fierce competition with one another. Every time the intelligence community has had a problem in the last thirty years, the ensuing revamp has only exacerbated it.

When I joined up, a senior officer from the Directorate of Operations came in and talked to our class on the first morning as we sat there nervously in a room in Arlington, Virginia. You will pride yourselves on the fact that you will never be more than three people away from the director of central intelligence, meaning the chief of station, the division chief, and the deputy director of operations, he said. By the time I retired, getting to see any DCI, including Tenet, was a major undertaking. Think Dorothy and the Wizard of Oz. And the yellow brick road just seemed to get longer and longer.

Even someone at my level, with the rank of Senior Intelligence Service 4—two rungs from the top—was separated from the top of the organization by a maze of special assistants and associate deputy directors. The Germans have a very appropriate word for this—a *Teufelskreis*—literally, a "devil's circle." And the more politics intruded into our work, the more labyrinthine the bureaucracy became; and the more labyrinthine our structure was, the easier it was for political motivations to put down roots and influence the work of intelligence gathering.

Sulick used to ask, "Do you think it was always this bad but we just didn't see it because we were too junior?" Or perhaps it's just like General Joseph Stilwell used to say—the higher a monkey climbs a pole, the more you see of his behind.

What we should learn from the horror of 9/11, as intelligence professionals, is that we need the flexibility to recognize that the terrorist issue differs from region to region and from country to country. If, for example, we focus only on senior Al Qaeda officials, we may find a strategic plan but miss the details of the operation as faceless men like Mohammed Atta carry them out. If we fall into this trap, we will once again be in the situation of knowing that there is a planned attack without having the operational details of the threat. There are no guarantees of our success, but we have to give ourselves the best chance to protect the American people. We have to fall back on tried and trusted methods of working our way into an organization from the bottom up, recruiting a low-level person who then brings along a more senior person. That is the only chance we have to penetrate a terrorist group whose members mistrust all outsiders.

After McLaughlin and I had announced our retirements, he once said to me, "The issue of how to deal with terrorism in the modern world is so important we should make it like a new Manhattan Project." I couldn't agree more. We should pull together the most brilliant minds in academia, the military, and intelligence, real experts in a group of manageable size, supported by the best minds in the computer industry. These people should define the scope and nature of the threat, and the goal, and work out a strategy that delineates everyone's role and responsibility. Simply saying that we are going to hunt down and kill or capture is not enough; this is a goal, not a policy.

As for the men and women of the CIA, we need to remember that most presidents come into office either fascinated by or scared of the agency. Neither attitude is healthy. With Iran-Contra, we could tell ourselves we were on the cutting edge of the Reagan doctrine. With the war on terrorism, we can say we are all going to get indicted one day but at least we'll have done our duty. That's not right, either. We have to strain to avoid drama, to find detachment. The drama should be in the work, in the reporting itself, not in the presentation of it at a president's briefing or the preparation of it. Another thing people are always vacillating about is whether we need generalists or specialists. We need neither. We need smart people who are flexible enough to learn technical subjects, for example about the intricacies of weapons programs, and to move through different cultures without sticking out like sore thumbs.

I am optimistic that our growing cooperation with European services will serve as an example to the U.S. government of how we can work discreetly with allies around the world to develop a policy for increased international participation that will allow us to address reconstruction and security problems in Iraq despite policy differences. I fear that if we maintain our current policy of depending on the military powering through these problems, our grandchildren will be fighting in that tragic land. And this seemingly endless struggle will only fuel the worldwide war on terror, as potential terrorists are drawn to the insurgency, where they receive combat experience that they can then bring to Europe and the United States.

One thing that gives me hope is that the American people seem to be waking up to the mistakes made by this administration. I sometimes think President Bush sees himself as a modern-day Abraham Lincoln. Few people remember how Lincoln suspended civilian courts and habeas corpus and set up military tribunals. They only remember that he saved the country. But this isn't the Civil War. As Lincoln himself once said, you can fool all of the people some of the time . . .

EPILOGUE

In the prologue, I shared with you the story of the *Los Angeles Times* reporter and how I learned that George Tenet and John McLaughlin had refused to acknowledge that they were informed of Curveball's unreliability. It bothered me to be at odds with Tenet. I like the man, even if I didn't always agree with how he ran things. He did a lot for me and really wanted to make a difference for the agency. My mother, who had never really recovered from my father's death from Parkinson's after devoting twenty-five years of her life to caring for him, used to worry about Tenet a lot. She was deteriorating when I returned from Europe, and spent a lot of time watching television, including Tenet's uncomfortable appearances before committees in Congress. My mother couldn't understand why he was being made a scapegoat. When Tenet asked about her, I would tell him she thought he was doing great. She was the salt of the earth and so this was a big compliment. When she had a bad heart attack in September 2003 and was in a country hospital at Hopewell near her home in Petersburg, Virginia, Tenet sent her a beautiful card, signing it "God bless." I took a week off to go down and see her when she was sick. I hadn't left the Washington area since the 9/11 attacks and it was a breath of fresh air to be in my hometown, where the machinations of the capital were of absolutely no importance. People there are accustomed to trusting their president, and it troubled me to hear the conviction with which they expressed their belief in the Bush administration.

A few months later, in summer 2004, right before Lord Butler issued a report on British intelligence failures on July 14 that blasted MI6 for its handling of sources, Tenet threw a dinner for Richard Dearlove, who had recently retired, though not, Downing Street insisted, because of Iraq. The dinner amounted to a British farewell for Tenet, who had given up his office a few days earlier.

It was a hot night, and the main lobby at headquarters was all rigged out with curtains. Someone said it looked a bit like a nightclub. After Tenet gave a stoic speech, his British counterpart took the floor and was highly emotional, particularly for an old intelligence professional. People who judge us have not done what we have done, he said, and then he gave Tenet a British medal of some kind.

Afterward Linda and I went up to him. I hadn't talked to him since the day he'd said he was leaving, so he hadn't heard that my mother had passed away in June. He looked genuinely shocked and physically shrank when he heard the bad news. Linda said something comforting—like, go and write a book and make your fortune. It sounds funny now, since I hadn't even thought about writing a book then. He just looked at her oddly.

I saw him only one more time after that, and he said I should drop by and see him, but I never have and I don't suppose I will now. He still has an office somewhere at Langley because people see him from time to time. At the party, Linda, who, since she left the agency, always feels like an outsider at these events, thought both he and Dearlove looked sad and defeated. But the former MI6 chief has a new life now, as master of Pembroke College at the University of Cambridge. I wonder if there is tension between them, bearing in mind the Downing Street memo and the Curveball debacle. The British government ended up just as tied up in knots as we were, and in some respects, even more so. The British service took it all even more badly than we did, perhaps because they are so much more accustomed to being allowed to function in secrecy, as we should be.

The other story I always remember when I think about Tenet relates to an officer in my division who was dying of a brain tumor. Tenet went to see him at his home in McLean right before he died and gave him a medal. I had appointed him special assistant, just to give him something to do, but he wasn't functioning well. On his last day at headquarters, he got lost. It was heartbreaking. His wife called up to say he was close to death, and that was when Tenet, Jack Downing, the deputy director for operations and our most respected case officer, and I went to see him. It was a strange sight as we drove up to his house, with Tenet's motorcade taking up much of the small McLean street. As Tenet gave him his medal, he also promoted him to the senior intelligence service, which meant more to this fellow than the medal. It was a true recognition of a life spent in dangerous places as he faced his death. Only a few people carry that rank. Believe it or not, some people at headquarters were actually irritated about that, thinking that somehow they would be disadvantaged. In truth the director always has a few promotions up his sleeve for times like this. I will never forget the look on the faces of my friend's wife and children. It was at moments like these that I thought Tenet had the makings of a truly great director. But despite his good heart, it seems to me he ended up being compromised by proximity to power. In my opinion, he committed a colossal error of judgment by failing to bring the intelligence being generated about weapons of mass destruction by people in my division to the attention of the president, either because he bought into their argument that Saddam had to be overthrown no matter what, or because he dismissed the reporting on Curveball and the Iraqi source without examining it closely enough.

It made me sad to see Tenet paraded before the nation like that, when the congressional committees grilled him about errors he could not reasonably be blamed for. When Bush gave Tenet the Medal of Freedom along with Paul Bremer, the former administrator of Iraq, and Tommy Franks, the whole scene stank of hypocrisy. Bush had been using Tenet as a lightning rod for so long that it was impossible to take the ceremony seriously. The Curveball story soured many relationships, including mine with McLaughlin. He was heroic in those months after Tenet left, after Porter Goss arrived. He finally retired after taking over temporarily as his deputy. But in the end, they do not want to admit they were wrong about Curveball. They know that my executive assistant kept all the documentation, though it is classified and I cannot share it with you. They know that I briefed James Pavitt and Steve Kappes on all the issues. I suppose I understand. They just can't bear their role.

The biggest problem with Tenet's statement about my testimony before the Silberman-Robb Commission is that there is corroboration for everything I have described about Curveball except the telephone call, which was nowhere near as important bureaucratically speaking as the meeting with McLaughlin. There is a pile of documents two feet high backing up my story. That is why the panel felt justified in repeating my account in their report. They concluded that Tenet and I remembered things differently, and that is the explanation I cling to today, even as the words of my old boss ring in my ears: "I have absolutely no recollection of the division chief saying anything to me with regard to problems with the foreign reporting."

Tenet said he had never heard about my meeting with my German counterpart Lothar, and that McLaughlin would have done "whatever was necessary" to ensure that unreliable information was kept out of Powell's speech had he been briefed on the concerns about Curveball. He described McLaughlin as a man known throughout his thirty-two-year career for his "professional discipline and meticulous care in evaluating the most difficult of issues." I don't disagree with that. That is what makes it all the more astonishing that Tenet appears to have been unaware of the concerns about Curveball. I am known for my memory. My colleagues always say that if I remember something, it happened. I'm sure I have remembered all the details about Curveball correctly.

As for Powell, he has said repeatedly that no one warned him about Curveball. In 2005 he gave an interview to the *Telegraph* in London saying he was very sore about the way his speech had worked out. "I will forever be known as the one who made the case," he said.* In June 2005, he appeared on the late-night comedian Jon Stewart's *Daily Show* and argued that a war could have been avoided if the international community had held firm with Saddam, and that Bush had decided in the end that if he failed to act, the moment would pass, and the Iraqi tyrant would wriggle out of the UN sanctions and stay in power. Everything the administration was being told by the intelligence community, he said, was "very disturbing." He recalled visiting the village of Halabja in northern Iraq where five thousand Kurds were killed in one morning. "This was not some academic exercise," he said. "We were concerned he would do that again." So why didn't the administration say so at the time, instead of trying to find a *casus belli* to go to war?

Powell's visit to Halabja, where Saddam gassed men, women, and children to death in a chemical attack in 1988, came months after the invasion, in September 2003. If the administration went to war on humanitarian grounds, it did not explain that to the American people, at least not until they had already realized that there were no stockpiles of weapons of mass destruction. This is particularly sad since the unilateral U.S. activities over the summer of 2002 had maneuvered the UN into a position where they would have moved against Saddam once they had completed the inspections.

Again, Powell blamed the intelligence community. His presentation was based entirely on information from us, as was the vote in Congress to approve the intervention, which took place after the release of that faulty National Intelligence Estimate.

*See *The Telegraph*, February 6, 2005.

Stewart, the late-night comedian, jumped in and asked Powell whether he hadn't had a call from anyone in Germany saying Curveball was kind of a "nut job." Powell didn't skip a beat and replied: "Not me. There may have been somebody who was called inside the system and said 'beware of Curveball,' but it never got to me and it never got to the president." His information, he said, had come directly from the director of central intelligence, not outside outfits like the Office of Special Plans at the Pentagon. I wonder what Tenet would say to that.

I think Powell, as an outsider, rather like Tenet, decided to pick his battles inside the administration carefully and, having persuaded Bush, with the help of the British, to go to the United Nations, lost control of the situation. But the stage had been set long before. There was an unbroken line at least from September 11, 2001, and probably from Bush's inauguration, to the day the bombs started to fall on Baghdad.

I have little sympathy for the argument that the troops were already in place and they would have had to sit in place for another year, so we had to go to war then or never. I bet any one of the nearly 2,700 Americans who have been killed would have gladly given up a year in the dirt rather than their lives. More than 20,000 Americans who have been injured in the conflict might well have traded a little discomfort for a missing limb, head injury, or other trauma.

For all his accomplishments, Powell will indeed forever be remembered as the man who held up a vial of fake anthrax, a silicone compound supplied by the agency, along with a load of inaccurate intelligence. I hope that he recognizes, as I do, that Tenet was not ultimately to blame. The men who are most to blame have never accepted responsibility and I don't suppose they ever will.

— —

It's been a tough transition from the CIA to the real world, for all three of us in my family. I miss the teamwork and the thrill of being with my friends, really the best friends anyone could have. The colleagues I have served beside are like brothers to me.

Livy was at a class sometime after my retirement. They were discussing the case of a State Department employee who'd resigned in protest at the Iraq War. "She was just about to retire anyway, wasn't she?" one of her fellow students said. Livy leaped in. "You just don't get it. You don't just do that," she said, thinking of me. "Why wasn't it in the news, then?" the student responded after she'd told a little of my story. How could she possibly explain? Sure, I'd been in the news. But the stories hardly scratched the surface of what we'd been through. After so many years, you'd think my family would grow accustomed to being misunderstood. Maybe it's a good thing that we never did.

In June 2005, I received my Distinguished Career Intelligence Medal in the mail, as I had requested. I didn't want any embarrassing ceremonies. I opened it up and fell into a bit of a reverie, reflecting on my career and the years past, the successes and the friends gained, the colleagues lost and the mistakes made.

But I'm enjoying my new career. I still get called to committee hearings from time to time, and testify willingly, continuing the tradition of service I inherited from my father and his father, and hoping that I can thereby continue to serve this country, to which I have dedicated, and will continue to dedicate, my life.

CO-AUTHOR'S NOTE

The material in the following sections was developed by Elaine Monaghan independent of any input from Tyler Drumheller. This step was taken to avoid accidentally revealing certain operational details that both Tyler and the CIA believe should be protected. The absence of these details does not affect the focus of this section, which is the story of the daily life of the Drumheller family during his career and their travels.

EPISODES FROM
THE LIFE OF
A CIA FAMILY

by Elaine Monaghan

Washington, D.C., late 1970s

It goes with the territory of Tyler's career that he cannot reveal exactly how it began, but it was the late 1970s when he was recruited by the Chinese professor mentioned in the book. Tyler was trying to pursue graduate school at Georgetown University by taking night courses while working during the day as a service representative for the Social Security Administration in southeast Washington. He had had a fascination with intelligence work since childhood, so it seemed like fate. His father was an Air Force chaplain who had entered the service in the early days of World War II and stayed on through Korea and Vietnam but had to retire in the late 1960s when he came down with Parkinson's.

In the early and mid-1960s, the family spent several years in Germany, and Tyler caught the travel bug early.

After arriving in Washington in the summer of 1974, he held his share of government jobs, raising funds for graduate studies by working as an intern at what was the Office of Education and then at the Social Security Administration. So it seemed like a natural progression.

The day he got the phone call to "start work," in Christmas week of 1979, was memorable for more than one reason. An outpatient at nearby St Elizabeth's, a hospital for the mentally ill, turned up at the Social Security Administration demanding his check. Tyler was trying to explain that it wasn't due for another week when the poor man leaped across the counter and grabbed him by the throat. He remembers asking a colleague to call the police. She got muddled up and dialed the wrong number. "411 doesn't answer! 411 doesn't answer!" she was screaming. "Call 911 for God's sake!" Tyler yelled.

He was really beginning to think the time had come to move on, even though he enjoyed that job because he thought he was making a difference. It had been months since he'd gone for his interview and polygraph at the agency, and he had all but given up on hearing anything, convinced he must have set off some trip wire with something he had said at the polygraph. Then the phone rang.

"Tyler," a voice said. "I'm calling to offer you the job."

"What job?" he asked. "Who is this?"

"The job that you were interviewed for, that you had the special tests for . . ."

Finally the penny dropped. He was so pleased that he forgot to ask how much he would be paid. It was only later, when his father asked, that he realized he had no idea. He thinks he ended up earning about $15,000 a year, which seemed like a fortune at the time. His father was unhappy that he had taken a two-week break between the Social Security Administration and starting at the CIA. "Have you got so much money you can afford not to work?" he asked. Tyler just couldn't believe that he was actually getting to follow his dream. His father's father had served in World War I and he felt like he was keeping up a family tradition.

He began his formal training in February of the following year. There were more than fifty people in the class. They were given a very dry overview of the CIA, with wiring diagrams. Tyler remembers turning around and scanning the room, wondering if he'd done the right thing. He later learned that those officers who would become his closest friends were asking themselves the same question. Some of them had had more colorful pasts than others; the group included former Navy SEALs. Tyler wasn't sure that he would fit in. They spent a lot of time on old skills that seemed designed to give them a link to the service's storied past while preparing them mentally and philosophically for the new challenges to come. They learned simple tasks such as opening safes, which reinforced the idea of office security while leaving them terrified they would leave something important lying out rather than locking it away. They were taken on a tour of all the departments. It was a little dull, but they were all looking forward to the next stage.

After this initial phase, Tyler joined an African desk for a six-week stint, followed by six weeks working on an operational desk. The East Asia division had been his obvious first interest, what with his Chinese studies, but he quickly discovered there was a whole string of Chinese Americans ahead of him whose mastery of the language was obviously far better than his own. He began to think he'd be better off in Africa, since it could otherwise take three years to leave American soil. The Chinese had stirred interest in that area by starting work on a railroad that would link Dar es Salaam in Tanzania with the copper belt in landlocked Zambia. Tyler's first branch chief—he thought he was the coolest guy he'd ever met, really smart, an eccentric, loved being a spy—was lining Tyler up to go to Africa in 1982.

Linda, who was working as a secretary in the Africa division, thought Tyler was an arrogant bonehead the first time they met, in the parking lot outside headquarters in November 1980. Tyler was filthy, unshaven, and exhausted after a tough week of training at The Farm. As he loaded a duffle bag with his belongings in the back of the car, he saw her walking past with a friend of his. He tried to engage her in conversation, but she wasn't terribly interested. He didn't realize she was stressed out because the friend, rather like Tyler, was chronically behind schedule; she is not, and she was complaining that he was going to make her late, again. "What's her problem?" Tyler asked his friend later.

Linda had joined the agency after answering an ad in the paper. She had been working in a bank in Carlisle, Pennsylvania. She and a co-worker went down to Harrisburg to take the test. Linda was invited to try out for a job as secretary. The FBI came down to the bank to check into her background. "Are you in trouble?" her boss asked nervously. Within a few weeks, she had started work. Nine months later, she was headed for Africa with Tyler. Her whole life changed in that time, and she wasn't always sure it was for the better.

If it hadn't been for her terrible Dodge Challenger, as they both often joke, they might never have married. She was earning about $10,000 a year and it was costing her hundreds of dollars every month to fix it. She would park on a hill and roll-start it. Tyler ran into her one day as she was about to walk to the highway to pick it up from the repair shop. He asked her if she needed a ride and she said yes. He then asked her what she was eating these days. Oh, you can buy these macaroni-and-cheese things in boxes, four for a dollar, and Heineken, and lots of eggs, she said. He took her to The Dubliner. He had his first credit card. They knew his name behind the bar. Things started to improve after that. They had their first real date on New Year's Eve.

Their fates were sealed soon afterward. There had been a series of expulsions of U.S. spies from Africa. The officer who was supposed to take over as deputy had been kicked out and couldn't return to the continent. This meant that Cofer Black, who was then the third officer, moved up to fill his shoes and there was now an opening in Africa. In March 1981, Tyler was asked to fill it. "Can I get back to you in a few minutes?" he asked his boss, who would also be his boss in Africa. "I have to ask Linda to marry me first."

So he took her to the third-floor stairwell and proposed. "Where's the ring," she asked. He hadn't bought one yet. "You're not even on your knees," she added. So Tyler got down on his knees, and she said yes. They went back to the office and called her mother, who was less than amused. Linda had been scheduled to go to Africa in 1982—they had to wait for her to turn twenty-one—and her mother was unprepared for the revised schedule.

Linda wasn't exactly prepared, either. She had to attend a weeklong personal protection program at The Farm. She learned how to shoot a gun, wreck a car, spot surveillance, and turn a vehicle at speed. The first thing she had to do was to take apart a gun. She'd never even seen one before. She started to cry. She'd never been out of the country or on a plane and there she was, in fatigues and army boots, dismantling a 9mm in preparation for life in Africa. She had to hang out the back of a car and shoot at passing targets, and learned how to handle an Uzi. She remembers being more than a little freaked out.

Tyler went home with her to Pennsylvania. Her father was cool about all of the news, and her mother was cool, too, in a different way. But she lightened up after a while when she saw Tyler was not a monster, as the couple recalls. They got married on June 20 in the Carlisle church where Linda's parents were married and she was baptized, by the same preacher. Tyler's father used his contacts to arrange for the rehearsal dinner at the Army War College in Carlisle barracks. At the reception, Linda overheard one of her great aunts being reassured by a colleague of Tyler's that "no one has been eaten by a lion in at least two or three months."

Their honeymoon lasted a week. It was at Cape May, New Jersey. Linda got food poisoning, so Tyler spent a fair bit of the time wandering the beach alone. They remember being poor as church mice and not owning a thing. Tyler's one smart outfit consisted of a blue jacket and khakis. Someone told him he would need a tuxedo for embassy receptions. He got a credit card for Garfinkel's, a D.C. department store. They gave him a $300 limit and the tuxedo cost $298. The store had shut down by the time he finally returned home, so it was the only thing he ever bought on that card. With the September departure date approaching, they tried to spend a long weekend with Tyler's best friend and college roommate at his home in Bermuda, but Tyler had to attend a course so he only got to stay one night. Linda took her sister with her and stayed longer. It was the beginning of many interruptions to their family life.

They had to buy four thousand pounds of food for the posting because African supplies were unreliable. They went to a massive warehouse in Fredericksburg, Virginia, and bought boxes and boxes of spaghetti, black olives, and pizza mix. Once they'd sorted out all their papers and shipped a car, they were ready to leave Washington. They spent a night at a hotel near National airport. Suddenly it started to feel like maybe they were on vacation, having a good time. The highlight was New York, where they spent three days while Tyler was taking a class and being briefed. Classes were finished by noon and they had money in their pockets for the first time in their lives. They ate at restaurants and stayed at the Hotel Pennsylvania opposite Madison Square Garden, where Tyler's parents had stayed forty years before en route to their first foreign tour. Linda is tough, but as their departure came closer she was really upset, Tyler recalls. *Evita* was playing and there were commercials for it every night on TV. The minute "Don't Cry for Me Argentina" came on, she would start to weep. The last night in the hotel, a rerun of *I Spy* with Bill Cosby and Robert Culp came on as Tyler sat up late contemplating their departure. It started to dawn on him that this was the real thing. People's lives would be in his hands. *You can't quit now,* he thought to himself.

The next day, six months after Tyler was first asked to go to Africa, the Drumhellers headed for Kennedy airport. "Don't worry," he told Linda, "if we don't like it, we'll do something else." Once they were on the plane, Linda was fine, and Tyler felt a rush of relief. He felt like they had finished a hurdles race. They had a layover in London. Prince Charles had just married Princess Diana, and the place was festooned. They felt good, like they were really on their way. The hotel was old-fashioned and had thin foam mattresses. The pipes showed in the bathroom. "If this is England," Linda said, "what's Africa going to be like?" "Don't worry," Tyler said, "it'll be like Bermuda." He was lying.

Predictably, the airline had technical difficulties and they ended up spending the night in the countryside somewhere while it was fixed. They left the next day. The plane, a 707, was packed with mining engineers. The emergency exit signs had OUT OF ORDER written on them with a marker. Fourteen hours later Tyler knew they were over Africa by the fires from the charcoal burners' compounds. As they arrived, the pilot reminded them to take malaria suppressants. Linda fell silent and did not utter a word for hours.

Lusaka, Zambia. September 1981

The night the Drumhellers arrived in their new home, they found a bottle of gin, a bottle of vodka, a casserole, and a snakebite kit in the fridge. The telephone and the radio weren't working. "You'll be all right until the morning," Tyler's new colleague John told him after meeting them at the airport. Abner, a local employee, was also there to welcome them. He fixed everything, like getting Tyler a driving license in return for two bottles of scotch. Whatever they paid him, as Tyler is apt to say, it wasn't enough.

Everywhere there was a smell as of body odor, from soldiers and more soldiers. They were everywhere at the airport, standing around wearing helmets and reflective sunglasses even though it was pitch black. Abner and John, who later became an ambassador in Africa, drove thirty miles, past a shantytown. Linda was just sitting there staring straight ahead, silent. John was scaring the hell out of both of them, talking about rabid dogs and crime and, when they got to the house, warning them to watch out for attackers who might strike in the time it took their guard to open the gate.

They went inside. It was a bungalow with a parquet floor. They had the smallest house around—a punishment, they always thought, for the fact that many in the embassy believed two of Tyler's colleagues had caused the expulsion of two diplomats by getting themselves exposed. Purple jacaranda trees surrounded them, making their eyes and noses weep. Tyler ate so many of the mangoes from the orchard in the backyard that he developed an allergy to them. The nurses at the embassy were wives of missionaries and appeared to believe in healing by prayer.

When they turned on the lights, the giant spiders and geckos hustled off. Bars covered the windows. A nine-foot-high cinderblock wall topped with broken glass bordered the garden. There were so many lights, the place looked like a baseball stadium. The house came with a staff of six who lived in a building on the grounds, John explained. As a parting note he informed the Drumhellers that the bars on the windows normally had hinges that would allow them to escape in the event of a fire, but their house didn't, so they had supplied bolt cutters. As the door closed behind Tyler, he stood there incredulously, holding the tool that could save their lives. Linda finally spoke her first words since arriving: "Where have you brought me?"

Then Bill, Tyler's new boss in Africa and old boss and mentor from headquarters, turned up. He took them out into the backyard. "Look at the stars," he said. "Look at the Southern Cross. Isn't this great?" By the time he left, Linda was OK.

The next morning, John picked Tyler up and he left twenty-one-year-old Linda with her new friends: Moses, the cook, and Dickson, the gardener; Sampson, an excellent guy with two thumbs on his right hand, which meant Africans wouldn't hire him; Blackson, the day guard; and Aideed, the night guard. He sang hymns to stay awake. A Seventh Day Adventist, he neither smoked nor drank, which made him a prize commodity as a night guard. He was from a tribe whose members were taller than the other tribes. They consider themselves the elite. Moses, who would make delicious beef Wellington for lunch unless he was asked for a tuna sandwich, was from a rival tribe, and the other three men were from a third tribe, the country's largest. One afternoon Moses got drunk and Dickson accused him of stealing whiskey. Linda was home alone, pregnant, and heard a commotion in the backyard. The men were all knocking lumps out of each other. The next thing she knew, Moses was trying to batter down the door. Linda, who for the first and last time picked up the gun in the house, was sitting on the bed facing the door, unaware that Moses was only trying to ask her not to tell Tyler he'd been drunk because he was afraid to lose his job.

Tyler always gets irritated when he hears people complain how risk averse the CIA has become, especially when he looks back at those years in Africa. Life was pretty safe, but even there the Drumhellers feel they faced risks every day. One night, Cofer Black, who had by then become the deputy head of the office, picked Tyler up for his first meeting. They sped through the empty streets in the pitch dark. When Tyler pointed out that he had been taught in training not to draw attention to himself, he recalls Cofer turned in mock-seriousness and said: "This is espionage." There were no other cars on the street, because everyone was afraid of having their vehicles stolen, so the only people out were the spies and the security service. Cofer screeched to a halt, told Tyler to get out, and pointed to the street corner where he was to make his first contact. As Cofer tore off, a local surveillance vehicle pulled up in the cross street and the three occupants turned and stared. Tyler thought for a second and then began walking back to the one European hotel in town, where Linda was supposed to meet him later. The trio followed him and did not see the poor contact, who was coming down the other street. As he walked he recalled the story of the diplomat who had been shot and killed the year before for not responding to a roadblock. The Social Security Administration didn't look so bad for a moment.

Eventually they met the contact, and he turned out to be tiny. Cofer, who is about 6'4", placed a huge cowboy hat on his head. He's more comfortable like this, Tyler remembers Cofer whispering, as if drowning the poor fellow in a massive hat would somehow draw attention away from him. Later the next year, while on leave in Virginia, Tyler recounted this story to his family. As the years went on he often looked back on that time, remembering how young and enthusiastic they had been. He and Linda really knew they were on the front line of the cold war, defending their friends and family from the advances of the "global adversary," the Soviet Union and its allies.

The cities of African countries were full of armed soldiers, guerrilla fighters and African National Congress forces, all hostile to the United States because they believed the United States was supporting the apartheid government in South Africa. It was the job of Tyler and his colleagues to find sources in all of these groups. Tyler recalls they did a terrific job of covering the government, but could have done better with the opposing forces. He feels they didn't concentrate as much as they should have on the ANC and the follow-on government until it was too late. Meeting the opposition figures was a tricky business because they were so closely followed by the authorities that pursuing contacts there would have meant execution for them and expulsion for the Americans. But Tyler often said they should have done more, despite the inherent difficulties on the ground.

As Tyler often says, everyone in his line of work starts out with misconceptions that can be dangerous and darkly comic. One night he was driving Bill, the boss, to a meeting with a contact from the South-west Africa People's Organization (SWAPO), in a particularly dark and dangerous part of town. Tyler was carrying a Browning 9mm but had no real desire to use it. As he returned to pick up Bill, he saw that two large Africans were following him. Fresh from The Farm, he could only think that he might compromise Bill, not that his boss might be about to have his throat slit for the contents of his pockets. Bill saw him start to speed up and screamed at him to stop as the pair began to run after Bill. Tyler came to his senses and picked Bill up.

Although it was certainly harder to penetrate terrorist groups than it was to make contacts on the diplomatic circuit, there are many lessons to be drawn from the Cold War in how the new generation of officers handles its interaction with potential agents and sources, Tyler believes. Mostly it requires forward planning and discipline—and a sense of humor. He handled several very sensitive cases that required him to meet agents in safe locations around town. Once, when leaving one of these houses through an alley gate, he saw a crowd of people carrying sticks and clubs coming at him. As he stood frozen to the spot, heart pounding, they ran straight past. He always chuckles as he recalls realizing they were chasing a thief!

Linda found out she was pregnant in February 1982. She went home to have their daughter Livy, who was born in October. Her parents came out to visit before she left and they all flew home together. Tyler was the officer for the airport, among his various duties, and it was rather terrifying watching the engineer cannibalize a part from another plane on the runway so his wife's plane could take off. He had a major operational triumph while she was away, partly thanks to a $1,600 liquor order Bill had made on their behalf for entertainment. ("You can pay me back," he said. Tyler had to call his mother to borrow the money.) Tyler recalls spending many a drunk, depressing night with the guy he was working with, whose wife was also back home having a baby. He had run into him at a supermarket where they could buy delicious sausage made by an Italian farmer who also produced pasta and cheese—until he was murdered. It was a classic African story of that time, and Tyler had asked why there was none of the sausage and cheese his new friend enjoyed so much. "The cheese is finished, the farmer is dead," the store worker had explained.

—-—

During that time, Vice President Bush came to Africa. As airport control officer, Tyler spent weeks working on his visit. Local authorities, who were supposedly neutral but actually on the hostile side, had a ceremonial cannon that they always used to fire in honor of important visitors. The Secret Service was going nuts at the mere idea of it and the deputy chief of mission and Tyler found themselves having to negotiate between the two sides. The officials agreed to fire the cannon from the other side of the airport. As the plane approached, Tyler could see the Secret Service talking down their sleeves into their radios to tell the plane what to expect. The lights were on. The plane was ready to land. He signaled to the commandant—Yodda was his name—and a huge ceremonial band struck up. The gumboot dancers started to shriek, complete with headdresses and stilts, and suddenly six guys in grenadier guard uniforms appeared and started dragging the cannon onto the runway. "What the hell is that?" the Secret Service guy was screaming. "Look, man, it's their country," Tyler said. They fired it and then wheeled it away, as the Secret Service looked on in silent fury.

A night one of the supply flights came in was the night Tyler almost died—at least he thinks he nearly did. He had to go out in the dead of night to wake the airport staff to guide the C-130 in. It was getting close to midnight, when the plane was due, and he was pounding on the door. Someone came out rubbing his eyes and went to put on the runway lights. By this time the plane was in touch, complaining they couldn't see where to land. Suddenly the guy pulled a massive switch, like something out of the Marx Brothers, and the whole place lit up like a Christmas tree. "Gosh!" the guy said, "I've never done that before!" The runway was covered with giant bats, which all took off at once.

Once they had dealt with a fueling problem—the Africans didn't like the pilot's credit card—Tyler headed off for home. He was missing Linda and had a big agent meeting the next day; he was going to have to get up early and it was nearly 3 A.M. Livy had already been born—she wouldn't arrive on African soil until she was six weeks old—and Tyler was feeling pretty sorry for himself. He drove through the gates and got out of the car, while his two German shepherds were going completely nuts. Moses and the others hated them because they used to eat the palm rats in the yard that they liked to fry up for lunch. Tyler felt something slap against his old baggy khakis. He looked down and saw a fluorescent green thing with big black eyes. It was a green mamba; it had just struck at him, and it was preparing to strike again. Tyler leaped backwards several feet, whereupon a dog grabbed the snake, threw it up in the air, and ate it. Tyler thought about that incident for a long time and often comments how ironic it is that of all the dangerous situations he has been in, it was a snake and not a human being that brought him closest to death.

—-

It was a tough time for Linda. There were no jobs available for her and the Drumhellers' social circle was very limited; they felt shunned by their colleagues because of the officer who'd been expelled. Events in Africa colored the entire tour, playing a part even in the timing of the Drumhellers' marriage. The couple was called in to deal with the aftermath of the expulsion incident. They had already gotten engaged, but this was the first time they really got to know one another, as they spent three days poring over the details and doing crisis management at headquarters.

While Tyler was dealing with all the drama at work, Linda had plenty of issues to address at home, including a crop of marijuana plants that mysteriously appeared in the midst of the corn their gardener grew. "Gosh, someone has planted dagga in the mealie patch!" he said. The embassy's head gardener, a rather humorless Polish émigré, had them removed.

They had one of their more memorable trips when Linda was seven months pregnant and their vehicle got stuck in the sand at a game park at sunset. Linda's father and mother were visiting and found it all very exciting. Linda's father suggested they should wait for the rangers, but earlier they had spotted them smoking joints at the gates so Tyler didn't hold out much hope for them. Tyler and Linda's parents got out and pushed, praying that the lions wouldn't come any closer.

There were times when the incongruity of their presence in such an impoverished country really hit home. Once, when Linda and Tyler were out collecting data for a cost-of-living report, a beggar decided to pursue Tyler and hit him over the head with a pipe. Tyler found it hard to blame him, under the circumstances. Another time, when Tyler was driving to meet a source, he and a friend who was riding with him saw a cow skull on the side of the road with a snake skin wrapped around its horns. They stopped to debate whether or not they should pick it up. "That's a real witchcraft sign," Tyler's friend said. "You've got to be joking," Tyler replied, "I've seen enough horror movies to know that's a really bad idea." To this day his friend complains about this incident and an opportunity missed. Tyler, on the other hand, has no regrets.

[**Publisher's note:** An anecdote concerning Africa was deleted here to satisfy CIA vetting requirements.]

——

Tyler and many of his colleagues remember this as an excellent time at the agency. Tyler feels he held a number of interesting jobs and learned something from desk officers and supervisors everywhere he went. The Africa division chief, Clare George, was highly experienced, and Tyler, like many of his colleagues, admired and respected him. Sadly and somewhat unfairly, as Tyler describes it, George later was caught up in the Iran-Contra affair. It wasn't just that he took time to talk to the trainees; he really believed in keeping short lines of command. Tyler went with him one time when he was a humble Africa desk officer to brief the deputy director of operations and senior management on an important issue. They went up in the elevator to see William Casey, the DCI. Such a thing would not happen now, Tyler says. Too many people have too much to lose from giving away an inch of bureaucratic ground.

He also felt very lucky to work with some excellent ambassadors. They understood the importance of what intelligence officers were doing, and, perhaps most importantly, didn't treat them like pariahs, Tyler recalls. One ambassador, Frank, always made sure Tyler fulfilled the obligations of his various jobs. So he had to spend time with an array of people, including the head of the local railways. It was good discipline.

[**Publisher's note:** An anecdote concerning Africa was deleted here to satisfy CIA vetting requirements.]

In Africa, Tyler and his colleagues had to meet contacts regularly, and this made for some tense experiences. The family remembers it as being particularly tough. Linda had to do a lot of late-night driving, ferrying between meetings, often with their daughter in the car.

This was a time when the government of a certain African country believed it was fighting for its existence. Tyler and his colleagues were under constant threat of death and imprisonment. One night he was involved in a bad car accident with a senior contact in the car. The risk to them both was not so much the crash as the possibility of being exposed to the police. Fortunately, they both made it out alive and free.

The family's three years in this country were made all the more difficult by the local security situation. Livy's nanny, Pauline, helped the Drumhellers keep their heads by laughing about it.

The family remembers some of the neighbors as being pretty vicious. One of them, an elderly gentleman, threatened during a particularly unpleasant conversation with Pauline to kill their little dog Scampi, a refugee from the pound. Linda told her to tell him that if anything happened to the dog, they would call the police and say he was the dog poisoner, a psycho who had been killing dogs throughout the city. Most Africans love dogs and he knew that he would be taken into custody while the matter was investigated. After that, as the family recalls, he always asked after the dog's health.

Linda had to deal with suspicion and aggression from all quarters, even in her civilian life. She was pushed out of line by local men, told to go home when women in a lingerie shop heard her accent after U.S. sanctions were imposed against the government, and had to watch Marie, an American friend, get thrown off a bus.

The day they picked Scampi up at the dog pound, police were picking up their gardener across the street from their house for not having his passbook. They took him to a police station, about ten miles away, and made him walk home.

On one particular trip the family remembers well, Tyler walked around the corner to the spot where he was due to meet Linda. She had had to make her way back by an unexpected route. She had somehow misjudged the time and was literally driving at 100 miles per hour to arrive at their meeting point at the same time. It was about 11 P.M. and he was standing on the street, waiting for her. She was upset and angry with herself when she arrived. Tyler was exhausted. Livy was snoozing in the backseat. They made it home in one piece.

As the Drumhellers lived with the day-to-day realities of local policy, it was becoming harder to keep a detached focus on the cold war aspects of the situation in Africa.

[**Publisher's note:** Anecdotes about Africa and the Drumhellers' return to life in the U.S. were deleted here to satisfy CIA vetting requirements.]

AFTERWORD

by Elaine Monaghan

I n the year since we finished the first draft of this book, Tyler has become something of a television celebrity, much to his bemusement. In the process, the media have cast a light on some of the stories contained in the chapters of this manuscript, which like anything written by a CIA retiree, have had to go through an exhaustive vetting process at the agency. It took many months, and we lost more than one sixth of the book in the process. The names of countries came back blacked out, including those of European allies whose intelligence services have been nothing but helpful to the United States since 9/11.

The goal of the vetting process is to protect the sources and methods used in the business of collecting intelligence. Tyler included as many pertinent recollections as he could of his experiences (and for the record, the quotes are obviously based on his memory of events, though we only included those he strongly believed matched the words uttered at the time). But he clearly had to exclude some details, including, as you have seen, the name of the Iraqi source, and the names of some countries whose cooperation he witnessed. He never complained, knowing that this was the result of a decision he made a long time ago to live his life in the service of the CIA.

For me, it was frustrating to know that some of the color in his stories had doubtless been erased, and to see him having to steer clear of topics I know he would have liked to dwell on in more detail.

[**Publisher's note:** Material about a *60 Minutes* investigation of the pre-invasion period in Iraq has been deleted to satisfy CIA vetting requirements.]

—

On the subject of renditions and torture, I would like to make it clear to the reader that Tyler is severely restricted in what he can say by the existence of ongoing investigations, although he tried to offer his opinion wherever possible on how these most difficult of issues should be handled.

In the past year, the media has turned with intensity to the subject of secret CIA detention facilities in Europe, anonymous CIA flights used to spirit suspects from country to country and ongoing cases of suspects who were allegedly seized from the streets of European countries. The international community will surely have to make tough decisions about the rights and wrongs of handling terrorist suspects. Tyler hopes that some of the insights he offers in these pages will help provide some perspective from a long-serving intelligence officer on these matters.

One of the messages to have emerged from the reporting is that there is a wide gap between what Western governments say and do in this regard. President Bush has bluntly claimed that the United States does not torture. European governments appear to be holding out the hope that if they do not criticize the United States too much for its tactics in the secret war against terrorism, they will not have to answer to their own populations for their apparent acquiescence—or even direct involvement—in this matter.

Yet there have been countless articles pointing to the use of "waterboarding" against American-held detainees. This method of torture involves strapping someone down and holding him or her under water for so long they believe they are going to die. Human rights organizations say that waterboarding practitioners sometimes place a towel over the face of the detainee and pour water over him or her to induce the sensation of drowning. Many men and women with experience in interrogation tactics firmly believe that the use of such extreme measures is not only counterproductive and potentially fatal but also quite likely to produce incorrect information. There have also been reports of three suspects dying in detention in Afghanistan, at least one of them as a result of waterboarding. We leave it to the reader to decide the moral rights and wrongs of using physical pain against a detainee whose guilt has not been established in any court of law.

Perhaps Tyler's most important point is that fostering good relations with allies is the single most effective way of preventing future terrorist attacks. In that regard it has been frustrating for him to have to conceal the identities of European countries that worked with the United States to avert terrorist attacks since the September 11 bloodshed.

In my own reading during the preparation of this book, I found it particularly fascinating to hear the tale of an operation in Paris known as the "Alliance Base." According to a long article on the subject by Dana Priest published in the *Washington Post* in November 2005, the CIA has established such joint operations centers in more than two dozen countries, allowing U.S. and foreign intelligence services to work side by side in an unprecedented fashion to unearth Al Qaeda and other terrorist suspects and decide whether to deliver them to other countries for interrogation.

Priest wrote that said the centers' computers were hooked up to CIA's central databases and gave access to highly classified intercepts that in the past had only been shared with America's closest Western allies.

[**Publisher's note:** A discussion here of detainee detention practices has been deleted to satisfy CIA vetting requirements.]

— —

I felt it would be worth including a section of the findings of the presidential commission chaired by Laurence H. Silberman and Charles S. Robb, released March 31, 2005 and available in full at http://www.wmd.gov/report/wmd_report.pdf. The chairmen, in a cover letter to the president, report that the intelligence community was "dead wrong in almost all of its pre-war judgments about Iraq's weapons of mass destruction," a conclusion that makes interesting reading in the light of Tyler's story. It pinned the blame for this failure on the community's "inability to collect good information about Iraq's WMD programs, serious errors in analyzing what information it could gather, and a failure to make clear just how much of its analysis was based on assumptions, rather than good evidence."

It added: "After a thorough review, the Commission found no indication that the Intelligence Community distorted the evidence regarding Iraq's weapons of mass destruction. What the intelligence professionals told you about Saddam Hussein's programs was what they believed. They were simply wrong." Tyler believes this conclusion falls short of presenting the full picture of what the community knew or was trying to find out about Saddam's capabilities.

The following section, taken from pages 83 to 110 of the nearly six-hundred-page report, addresses the case of Curveball in detail. It uses the following acronyms, listed below in order of appearance unless they are already explained in the text:

BW—biological weapons

DIA—Defense Intelligence Agency

HUMINT—human intelligence

NIE—National Intelligence Estimate

IC—Intelligence Community

WINPAC—Weapons Intelligence, Non-Proliferation, and Arms Control Center

DCI—Director of Central Intelligence

CW—Chemical Weapons

UNSCOM—United Nations Special Commission

DO—Directorate of Operations (CIA)

DDCI—Deputy Director of Central Intelligence

INR—Bureau of Intelligence and Research (Department of State)
DI—Directorate of Intelligence (CIA)

Growing concern. The Intelligence Community's concern about Iraq's BW program increased in early 2000, and the Community began to adjust upward its estimates of the Iraq BW threat, based on a "substantial volume" of "new informa-tion" regarding mobile BW facilities in Iraq. This information came from an Iraqi chemical engineer, subsequently code-named Curveball, who came to the attention of the Intelligence Community through a foreign liaison service. That liaison service debriefed Curveball and then shared the debriefing results with the United States. The foreign liaison service would not, however, provide the United States with direct access to Curveball. Instead, information about Curveball was passed from the liaison service to DIA's Defense HUMINT Service, which in turn disseminated information about Curveball throughout the Intelligence Community.

Between January 2000 and September 2001, DIA's Defense HUMINT Service disseminated almost 100 reports from Curveball regarding mobile BW facilities in Iraq. These reports claimed that Iraq had several mobile production units and that one of those units had begun production of BW agents as early as 1997.

Shortly after Curveball started reporting, in the spring of 2000, his information was provided to senior policymakers. It was also incorporated into an update to a 1999 NIE on World-wide BW Programs. The update reported that "new intelligence acquired in 2000 . . . causes [the IC] to adjust our assessment upward of the BW threat posed by Iraq . . . The new information suggests that Baghdad has expanded its offensive BW pro-gram by establishing a large-scale, redundant, and concealed BW agent production capability."In December 2000, the Intelligence Community produced a Special Intelligence Report that was based on reporting from Curveball, noting that "credible reporting from a single source suggests" that Iraq has produced biological agents, but cautioned that "[w]e cannot confirm whether Iraq has produced . . . biological agents."

By 2001, however, the assessments became more assertive. A WINPAC report in October 2001, also based on Curveball's reporting about mobile facilities, judged "that Iraq continues to produce at least . . . three BW agents" and possibly two others. This assessment also concluded that "the establishment of mobile BW agent production plants and continued delivery system development provide Baghdad with BW capabilities sur-passing the pre-Gulf War era." Similar assessments were provided to senior policymakers. In late September 2002, DCI Tenet told the Senate's Intelligence and Armed Services Committees (and subsequently the Senate Foreign Relations Committee) that "we know Iraq has developed a redundant capability to produce biological warfare agents using mobile production units."

October 2002 NIE. The October 2002 NIE reflected this upward assessment of the Iraqi BW threat that had devel-oped since Curveball began reporting in January 2000. The October 2002 NIE reflected the shift from the late-1990s assessments that Iraq *could* have biological weapons to the definitive conclusion that Iraq "has" biological weapons, and that its BW program was larger and more advanced than before the Gulf War. Information about Iraq's dual-use facilities and its failure to account fully for previously declared stock-piles contributed to this shift in assessments. The information that Iraq had mobile BW production units, however, was instrumental in adjusting upward the assessment of Iraq's BW threat. And for this conclusion, the NIE relied primarily on reporting from Curveball, who, as noted, provided a large volume of reporting through Defense HUMINT channels regarding mobile BW production facilities in Iraq. Only in May 2004, more than a year after the commencement of Opera-tion Iraqi Freedom, did CIA formally deem Curveball's reporting fabricated and recall it. At the time of the NIE, how-ever, reporting from three other human sources—who pro-vided one report each on mobile BW facilities—was thought to have corroborated Curveball's information about the mobile facilities. These three sources also proved problem-atic, however, as discussed below.

Another asylum seeker (hereinafter "the second source") reporting through Defense HUMINT channels provided one report in June 2001 that Iraq had transportable facilities for the production of BW. This second source recanted in October 2003, however, and the recantation was reflected in a Defense HUMINT report in which the source flatly contradicted his June 2001 statements about transportable facilities.250 Though CIA analysts told Commission staff that they had requested that Defense HUMINT follow-up with this second source to ascer-tain the reasons for his recantation, DIA's Defense HUMINT Service has provided no further information on this issue. Nor, for that matter, was the report ever recalled or corrected.

Another source, associated with the Iraqi National Congress (INC) (hereinafter "the INC source"), was brought to the attention of DIA by Washington-based representatives of the INC. Like Curveball, his reporting was handled by Defense HUMINT. He provided one report that Iraq had decided in 1996 to establish mobile laboratories for BW agents to evade inspectors. Shortly after Defense HUMINT's initial debriefing of the INC source in February 2002, however, a foreign liaison service and the CIA's Directorate of Operations (DO) judged him to be a fabricator and recommended that Defense HUMINT issue a notice to that effect, which Defense HUMINT did in May 2002. Senior policymakers were informed that the INC source and his reporting were unreliable. The INC source's information, however, began to be used again in finished intelligence in July 2002, including the October 2002 NIE, because, although a fabrication notice had been issued several months earlier, Defense HUMINT had failed to recall the reporting.

The classified report here discusses a fourth source (hereinafter "the fourth source") who provided a single report that Iraq had mobile fermentation units mounted on trucks and railway cars.

Post-NIE. After publication of the NIE in October 2002, the Intelligence Community continued to assert that Baghdad's biological weapons program was active and posed a threat, relying on the same set of sources upon which the NIE's judgments were based. For example, a November 2002 paper produced by CIA's Directorate of Intelligence (DI) reiterated the NIE's assessment that Iraq had a "broad range of lethal and incapacitating agents" and that the "BW program is more robust than it was prior to the Gulf War." The piece contended that Iraq was capable of producing an array of agents and probably retained strains of the smallpox virus. It further argued that technological advances increased the potential Iraqi BW threat to U.S. interests. And a February 2003 CIA Intelligence Assessment anticipated Iraqi options for BW (and CW) use against the United States and other members of the Coalition; the report stated that Iraq "maintains a wide range of . . . biological agents and delivery systems" and enumerated 21 BW agents which it judged Iraq could employ.

Statements about biological weapons also appeared in Administration statements about Iraq in the months preceding the war. Secretary of State Colin Powell's speech to the United Nations Security Council on February 5, 2003, relied on the same human sources relied upon in the NIE. Secretary Powell was not informed that one of these sources—the INC source— had been judged a fabricator almost a year earlier. And as will be discussed at length below, serious doubts about Curveball had also surfaced within CIA's Directorate of Operations at the time of the speech—but these doubts also were not communicated to Secretary Powell before his United Nations address.

Reliance on Curveball's reporting also affected post-war assessments of Iraq's BW program. A May 2003 CIA Intelligence Assessment pointed to the post-invasion discovery of "two probable mobile BW agent productions plants" by Coalition forces in Iraq as evidence that "Iraq was hiding a biological warfare program." Curveball, when shown photos of the trailers, identified components that he said were similar to those on the mobile BW production facilities that he had described in his earlier reporting.

Post-war Findings of the Iraq Survey Group
The Iraq Survey Group found that the Intelligence Community's pre-war assessments about Iraq's BW program were almost

entirely wrong. The ISG concluded that "Iraq appears to have destroyed its undeclared stocks of BW weapons and probably destroyed remaining holdings of bulk BW agent" shortly after the Gulf War. According to the ISG, Iraq initially intended to retain elements of its biological weapons program after the Gulf War. UNSCOM inspections proved unexpectedly intrusive, however, and to avoid detection, Saddam Hussein ordered his son-in-law and Minister of the Military Industrial Commission Hussein Kamil to destroy, unilaterally, Iraq's stocks of BW agents. This took place in either the late spring or summer of 1991. But Iraq retained a physical plant at Al-Hakam and the intellectual capital necessary to resuscitate the BW program. Simultaneously, Iraq embarked on an effort to hide this remaining infrastructure and to conceal its pre-war BW-related activities.

In early 1995, however, UNSCOM inspectors confronted Iraqi officials with evidence of 1988 imports of bacterial growth media in quantities that had no civilian use within Iraq's limited biotechnology industry. This confrontation, followed by the defection of Hussein Kamil in August 1995, prompted Iraq to admit that it had produced large quantities of bulk BW agent before the Gulf War. Iraq also released a large cache of documents and issued the first of several "Full, Final and Complete Declaration[s]" on June 22, 1996, further detailing its BW program. UNSCOM subsequently supervised the destruction of BW-related facilities at Al-Hakam in 1996.

The Iraq Survey Group found that the destruction of the Al-Hakam facility effectively marked the end of Iraq's large-scale BW ambitions. The ISG did judge that after 1996 Iraq "continued small-scale BW-related efforts" under the auspices of the Iraqi Intelligence Service, and also retained a trained cadre of scientists who could work on BW programs and some dual-use facilities capable of conversion to small-scale BW agent production.

Nevertheless, the ISG "found no direct evidence that Iraq, after 1996, had plans for a new BW program or was conducting BW-specific work for military purposes."

With respect to mobile BW production facilities, the "ISG found no evidence that Iraq possessed or was developing production systems on road vehicles or railway wagons." The ISG's "exhaustive investigation" of the two trailers captured by Coalition forces in spring 2003 revealed that the trailers were "almost certainly designed and built exclusively for the generation of hydrogen." The ISG judged that the trailers "cannot . . . be part of any BW program."

Analysis of the Intelligence
Community's Pre-war Assessments

The Intelligence Community fundamentally misjudged the status of Iraq's BW programs. As the above discussion demonstrates, the central basis for the Intelligence Community's pre-war assessments about Iraq's BW program was the reporting of a single human source, Curveball. This single source, whose reporting came into question in late 2002, later proved to be a fabricator.

Our intelligence agencies get burned by human sources sometimes—it is a fact of life in the murky world of espionage. If our investigation revealed merely that our Intelligence Community had a source who later turned out to be lying, despite the best tradecraft practices designed to ferret out such liars, that would be one thing. But Curveball's reporting became a central part of the Intelligence Community's pre-war assessments through a serious breakdown in several aspects of the intelligence process. The Curveball story is at the same time one of poor asset validation by our human collection agencies; of a tendency of analysts to believe that which fits their theories; of inadequate communication between the Intelligence Community and the policymakers it serves; and, ultimately, of poor leadership and management. This section thus focuses primarily on our investigation of the Curveball episode, and the findings we drew from it.

The problems with the Intelligence Community's performance on Curveball began almost immediately after the source first became known to the U.S. government in early 2000. As noted above, Curveball was not a source who worked directly with the United States; rather, the Intelligence Community obtained information about Curveball through a foreign service. The foreign service would not provide the United States with direct access to Curveball, claiming that Curveball would refuse to speak to Americans. Instead, the foreign intelligence service debriefed Curveball and passed the debriefing information to DIA's Defense HUMINT Service, the human intelligence collection agency of the Department of Defense.

The lack of direct access to Curveball made it more difficult to assess his veracity. But such lack of access does not preclude the Intelligence Community from attempting to assess the source's bona fides and the credibility of the source's reporting. Indeed, it is incumbent upon professional intelligence officers to attempt to do so, through a process referred to within the Intelligence Community as "vetting" or "asset validation."

Defense HUMINT, however, did not even attempt to determine Curveball's veracity. A Defense HUMINT official explained to Commission staff that Defense HUMINT believed that it was just a "conduit" for Curveball's reporting—that it had no responsibility for vetting Curveball or validating his information. In Defense HUMINT's view, asset validation is solely the responsibility of analysts—in their judgment if the analysts believe the information is credible, then the source is validated. This line echoes what Defense HUMINT officials responsible for disseminating Curveball's reporting told the Senate Select Committee on Intelligence; they told the Committee that it was not their responsibility to assess the source's credibility, but that it instead was up to the analysts who read the reports to judge the accuracy of the contents.

The Senate Select Committee on Intelligence concluded that this view represents a "serious lapse" in tradecraft, and we agree. Analysts obviously play a crucial role in validating sources by evaluating the credibility of their reporting, corroborating that reporting, and reviewing the body of reporting to ensure that it is consistent with the source's access. But analysts' validation can only extend to whether what a source says is internally consistent, technically plausible, and credible given the source's claimed access. The process of validation also must include efforts by the operational elements to confirm the source's bona fides (i.e., authenticating that the source has the access he claims), to test the source's reliability and motivations, and to ensure that the source is free from hostile control. To be sure, these steps are particularly difficult for a source such as Curveball, to whom the collection agency has no direct access. But human intelligence collectors can often obtain valuable information weighing on even a liaison source's credibility, and the CIA's DO routinely attempts to determine the credibility even of sources to whom it has no direct access. In light of this, we are surprised by the Defense HUMINT's apparent position that it had no responsibility even to *attempt* to validate Curveball.

As a footnote to this episode, while DIA's Defense HUMINT Service felt no obligation to vet Curveball or validate his veracity, it would later appear affronted that another agency—CIA—would try to do so. On February 11, 2003, after questions about Curveball's credibility had begun to emerge, an element of the DO sent a message to Defense HUMINT officials expressing concern that Curveball had not been vetted. The next day the Defense HUMINT division chief who received that message forwarded it by electronic mail to a subordinate, requesting input to answer CIA's query. In that electronic mail message, the Defense HUMINT division chief said he was "shocked" by CIA's suggestion that Curveball might be unreliable. The reply—which the Defense HUMINT official intended for Defense HUMINT recipients only but which was inadvertently sent to CIA as well—observed that "CIA is up to their old tricks" and that CIA did not "have a clue" about the process by which Curveball's information was passed from the foreign service.

As we have discussed, when information from Curveball first surfaced in early 2000, Defense HUMINT did nothing to validate Curveball's reporting. Analysts within the Intelligence Community, however, did make efforts to assess the credibility of the information provided by Curveball. In early 2000, when Curveball's reporting first surfaced, WINPAC analysts researched previous reporting and concluded that Curveball's information was plausible based upon previous intelligence, including imagery reporting, and the detailed, technical descriptions of the mobile facilities he provided. As a WINPAC BW analyst later told us, there was nothing "obviously wrong" with Curveball's information, and his story—that Iraq had moved to a mobile capability for its BW program in 1995 in order to evade inspectors—was logical in light of other known information.

At about the same time, however, traffic in the CIA's Directorate of Operations began to suggest some possible problems with Curveball. The first CIA concerns about Curveball's reliability arose within the DO in May 2000, when a Department of Defense detailee assigned to the DO met Curveball. The purpose of the meeting was to evaluate Curveball's claim that he had been present during a BW accident that killed several of his coworkers by seeing whether Curveball had been exposed to, or vaccinated against, a BW agent. Although the evaluation was ultimately inconclusive, the detailee raised several concerns about Curveball based on their interaction.

First, the detailee observed that Curveball spoke excellent English during their meeting. This was significant to the detailee because the foreign service had, on several earlier occasions, told U.S. intelligence officials that one reason a meeting with Curveball was impossible was that Curveball did not speak English. Second, the detailee was concerned by Curveball's apparent "hangover" during their meeting. The detailee conveyed these impressions of Curveball informally to CIA officials, and WINPAC BW analysts told Commission staff that they were aware that the detailee was concerned that Curveball might be an alcoholic. This message was eventually re-conveyed to Directorate of Operations supervisors via electronic mail on February 4, 2003—literally on the eve of Secretary Powell's speech to the United Nations. The electronic mail stated, in part:

> I do have a concern with the validity of the information based on Curveball having a terrible hangover the morning of [the meeting]. I agree, it was only a one time interaction, however, he knew he was to have a [meeting] on that particular morning but tied one on anyway. What underlying issues could this be a problem with and how in depth has he been vetted by the [foreign liaison service]?

By early 2001, the DO was receiving operational messages about the foreign service's difficulties in handling Curveball, whom the foreign service reported to be "out of control," and whom the service could not locate. This operational traffic regarding Curveball was shared with WINPAC's Iraq BW analysts because, according to WINPAC analysts, the primary BW analyst who worked on the Iraq issue had close relations with the DO's Counterproliferation Division (the division through which the operational traffic was primarily handled). This and other operational information was not, however, shared with analysts outside CIA.

A second warning on Curveball came in April 2002, when a foreign intelligence service, which was also receiving reporting from Curveball, told the CIA that, in its view, there were a variety of problems with Curveball. The foreign service began by noting that they were "inclined to believe that a significant part of [Curveball's] reporting is true" in light of his detailed technical descriptions. In this same message, however, the foreign service noted that it was "not convinced that Curveball is a wholly reliable source," and that "elements of [Curveball's] behavior strike us as typical of individuals we would normally assess as fabricators." Even more specifically, the foreign service noted several inconsistencies in Curveball's reporting which caused the foreign service "to have doubts about Curveball's reliability." It should be noted here that, like the handling foreign service, this other service continued officially to back Curveball's reporting throughout this period.

Again, these concerns about Curveball were shared with CIA analysts working on the BW issue. But none of the expressed concerns overcame analysts' ultimate confidence in the accuracy of his information. Specifically, analysts continued to judge his information credible based on their assessment of its detail and technical accuracy, corroborating documents, confirmation of the technical feasibility of the production facility designs described by Curveball, and reporting from another human source, the fourth source mentioned above. But it should be noted that during the pre-NIE period—in addition to the more general questions about Curveball's credibility discussed above—at least some evidence had emerged calling into question the substance of Curveball's reporting about Iraq's BW program as well.

Specifically, a WINPAC BW analyst told us that two foreign services had both noted in 2001 that Curveball's description of the facility he claimed was involved in the mobile BW program was contradicted by imagery of the site, which showed a wall across the path that Curveball said the mobile trailers traversed. Intelligence Community analysts "set that information aside," however, because it could not be reconciled with the rest of Curveball's information, which appeared plausible.

Analysts also explained away this discrepancy by noting that Iraq had historically been very successful in "denial and deception" activities and speculated that the wall spotted by imagery might be a temporary structure put up by the Iraqis to deceive U.S. intelligence efforts.

Analysts' use of denial and deception to explain away discordant evidence about Iraq's BW programs was a recurring theme in our review of the Community's performance on the BW question. Burned by the experience of being wrong on Iraq's WMD in 1991 and convinced that Iraq was restarting its programs, analysts dismissed indications that Iraq had actually abandoned its prohibited programs by chalking these indicators up to Iraq's well-known denial and deception efforts. In one instance, for example, WINPAC analysts described reporting from the second source indicating Iraq was filling BW warheads at a transportable facility near Baghdad. When imagery was unable to locate the transportable BW systems at the reported site, analysts assumed this was not because the activity was not taking place, but rather because Iraq was hiding activities from U.S. satellite overflights. This tendency was best encapsulated by a comment in a memorandum prepared by the CIA for a senior policymaker: "Mobile BW information comes from [several] sources, one of whom is credible and the other is of undetermined reliability. We have raised our collection posture in a bid to locate these production units, but years of fruitless searches by UNSCOM indicate they are well hidden." Again, the analysts appear never to have considered the idea that the searches were fruitless because the weapons were not there.

The Community erred in failing to highlight its overwhelming reliance on Curveball for its BW assessments. The NIE judged that Iraq "has transportable facilities for producing bacterial and toxin BW agents" and attributed this judgment to multiple sources.

In reality, however, on the topic of mobile BW facilities Curveball provided approximately 100 detailed reports on the subject, while the second and fourth sources each provided a single report. (As will be discussed in greater detail below, the reporting of another source—the INC source—had been deemed a fabrication months earlier, but nonetheless found its way into the October 2002 NIE.) The presentation of the material as attributable to "multiple sensitive sources," however, gave the impression that the support for the BW assessments was more broadly based than was in fact the case. A more accurate presentation would have allowed senior officials to see just how narrow the evidentiary base for the judgments on Iraq's BW programs actually was.

Other contemporaneous assessments about Iraq's BW program also reflect this problem. For example, the Intelligence Community informed senior policymakers in July 2002 that CIA judged that "Baghdad has transportable production facilities for BW agents . . . according to defectors." Again, while three "defector" sources (Curveball, the second source, and the INC source) are cited in this report, Curveball's reporting was the overwhelmingly predominant source of the information.

And the NIE should not only have emphasized its reliance on Curveball for its BW judgments; it should also have communicated the limitations of the source himself. The NIE, for instance, described him as "an Iraqi defector deemed credible by the [Intelligence Community]." The use of the term "credible" was apparently meant to imply only that Curveball's reporting was technically plausible. To a lay reader, however, it implied a broader judgment as to the source's general reliability. This description obscured a number of salient facts that, given the Community's heavy reliance upon his reporting, would have been highly important for policymakers to know—including the fact that the Community had never gained direct access to the source and that he was known at the time to have serious handling problems. While policymakers may still have credited his reporting, they would at least have been warned about the risks in doing so.

After the NIE was published, but before Secretary Powell's speech to the United Nations, more serious concerns surfaced about Curveball's reliability. These concerns were never brought to Secretary Powell's attention, however. Precisely how and why this lapse occurred is the subject of dispute and conflicting memories. This section provides only a brief summary of the key events in this complicated saga.

The NIE went to press in early October 2002, but its publication did not end the need to scrutinize Curveball's reliability. To improve the CIA's confidence in Curveball, the CIA's Deputy Director for Operations (DDO), James Pavitt, sought to press the foreign intelligence service for access to Curveball.

Mr. Pavitt's office accordingly asked the chief ("the division chief") of the DO's regional division responsible for relations with the liaison service ("the division") to meet with a representative of the foreign intelligence service to make the request for access. According to the division chief, he met with the representative in late September or early October 2002.

At the lunch, the division chief raised the issue of U.S.

intelligence officials speaking to Curveball directly. According to the division chief, the representative of the foreign intelligence service responded with words to the effect of "You don't want to see him [Curveball] because he's crazy." Speaking to him would be, in the representative of the foreign service's words, "a waste of time." The representative, who said that he had been present for debriefings of Curveball, continued that his intelligence service was not sure whether Curveball was actually telling the truth and, in addition, that he had serious doubts about Curveball's mental stability and reliability; Curveball, according to the representative, had had a nervous breakdown. Further, the representative said that he worried that Curveball was "a fabricator." The representative cautioned the division chief, however, that the foreign service would publicly and officially deny these views if pressed. The representative told the division chief that the rationale for such a public denial would be that the foreign service did not wish to be embarrassed. According to the division chief, he passed the information to three offices: up the line to the office of CIA's Deputy Director for Operations; down the line to his staff, specifically the division's group chief ("the group chief") responsible for the liaison country's region; and across the agency to WINPAC. At the time, the division chief thought that the information was "no big deal" because he did not realize how critical Curveball's reporting was to the overall case for Iraqi possession of a biological weapons program. He assumed there were other streams of reporting to buttress the Intelligence Community's assessments. He could not imagine, he said, that Curveball was "it."

Several months later, prompted by indications that the

President or a senior U.S. official would soon be making a speech on Iraq's WMD programs, one of the executive assistants for the then-Deputy Director of Central Intelligence (DDCI) John McLaughlin met with the group chief to look into the Curveball information. This meeting took place on December 18, 2002. Although the executive assistant did not specifically recall the meeting when he spoke with Commission staff, an electronic mail follow-up from the meeting—which was sent to the division chief and the group chief—makes clear that the meeting was called to discuss Curveball and the public use of his information.

As a result of this meeting, the division sent a message that same afternoon to the CIA's station in the relevant country again asking that the foreign intelligence service permit the United States to debrief Curveball. The message stressed the importance of gaining access to Curveball, and noted the U.S. government's desire to use Curveball's reporting publicly. On December 20, the foreign service refused the request for access, but concurred with the request to use Curveball's information publicly—"with the expectation of source protection."

By this point, it was clear that the division believed there was a serious problem with Curveball that required attention. A second meeting was scheduled on December 19 at the invitation of DDCI McLaughlin's same executive assistant. According to the executive assistant, he called the meeting because it had become apparent to DDCI McLaughlin that Curveball's reporting was significant to the Intelligence Community's judgments on Iraq's mobile BW capability. The invitation for the meeting stated that the purpose was to "resolve precisely how we judge Curveball's reporting on mobile BW labs," and that the executive assistant hoped that after the meeting he could "summarize [the] conclusions in a short note to the DDCI." The meeting was attended by the executive assistant, a WINPAC BW analyst, an operations officer from the DO's Counterproliferation Division, and the regional division's group chief. Mr. McLaughlin, who did not attend this meeting, told this Commission that he was not given a written summary of the meeting and did not recall whether any such meeting was held.

Although individuals' recollections of the meeting vary somewhat, there is little disagreement on the meeting's substance. The group chief argued that Curveball had not been adequately "vetted" and that his information should therefore not be relied upon. In preparation for the meeting, the group chief had outlined her concerns in an electronic mail to several officers within the Directorate of Operations—including Stephen Kappes, the then-Associate Deputy Director for Operations. The electronic mail opened with the following (in bold type):

> Although no one asked, it is my assessment that Curve Ball had some access to some of this information and was more forthcoming and cooperative when he needed resettlement assistance; now that he does not need it, he is less helpful, possibly because when he was being helpful, he was embellishing, a bit. The [foreign service] ha[s] developed some doubts about him. We have been unable to vet him operationally and know very little about him. The intelligence community has corroborated portions of his reporting with open source information . . . and some intelligence (which appears to confirm that things are where he said they were).

At the meeting, the group chief stated that she told the attendees that the division's concerns were based on the foreign service representative's statements to the division chief, the CIA's inability to get access to Curveball, the significant "improvement" in Curveball's reporting over time, the decline of Curveball's reporting after he received the equivalent of a green card, among other reasons. She also recalled telling the attendees the details of the foreign service representative's statements to the division chief. In the group chief's view, she made it clear to all the attendees that the division did not believe that Curveball's information should be relied upon.

With equal vigor, the WINPAC representative argued that Curveball's reporting was fundamentally reliable. According to the WINPAC analyst, Curveball's information was reliable because it was detailed, technically accurate, and corroborated by another source's reporting.

Both the group chief and the WINPAC analyst characterized the exchange as fairly heated. Both of the two primary participants also recalled providing reasons why the other's arguments should not carry the day. Specifically, the group chief says she argued, adamantly, that the supposedly corroborating information was of dubious significance because it merely established that Curveball had been to the location, not that he had any knowledge of BW activities being conducted there. In addition, the group chief questioned whether some of Curveball's knowledge could have come from readily available, open source materials. Conversely, the WINPAC BW analyst says that she questioned whether the group chief had sufficient knowledge of Curveball's reporting to be able to make an accurate assessment of his reliability.

It appears that WINPAC prevailed in this argument. Looking

back, the executive assistant who had called the meeting offered his view that the WINPAC BW analyst was the "master of [the Curveball] case," and that he "look[ed] to her for answers." He also noted that the group chief clearly expressed her skepticism about Curveball during the meeting, and that she fundamentally took the position that Curveball's reporting did not "hold up." The executive assistant further said that while the foreign service officially assessed that Curveball was reliable, they also described him as a "handling problem." According to the executive assistant, the foreign service said Curveball was a handling problem because he was a drinker, unstable, and generally difficult to manage. In the executive assistant's view, however, it was impossible to know whether the foreign service's description of Curveball was accurate. Finally, the executive assistant said that he fully recognized Curveball's significance at the time of the meeting; that Curveball "was clearly the most significant source" on BW; and that if Curveball were removed, the BW assessment was left with one other human source, "but not much more."

The following day, the executive assistant circulated a memorandum to the WINPAC BW analyst intended to summarize the prior day's meeting. Perhaps in keeping with his reliance on the WINPAC BW analyst as the "master of the case," the executive assistant's summary of the draft of the memorandum, titled "Reliability of Human Reporting on Iraqi Mobile BW Capability," played down the doubts raised by the DO division:

> The primary source of this information is an Iraqi émigré (vice defector) . . . After an exhaustive review, the U.S. Intelligence Community—[as well as several liaison services] . . . judged him credible. This judgment was based on:

- The detailed, technical nature of his reporting;
- [Technical intelligence] confirming the existence/ configuration of facilities he described (one Baghdad office building is known to house administrative offices linked to WMD programs);
- UNSCOM's discovery of military documents discussing "mobile fermentation" capability;
- Confirmation/replication of the described design by U.S. contractors (it works); and
- Reporting from a second émigré that munitions were loaded with BW agent from a mobile facility parked within an armaments center south of Baghdad.

The memorandum then continued on to note that "[w]e are handicapped in efforts to resolve legitimate questions that remain about the source's veracity and reporting because the [foreign service] refuses to grant direct access to the source." Later, in the "Questions/Answers" section, the memorandum stated:

> **How/when was the source's reliability evaluated—**
> [One foreign service] hosted a . . . meeting in 2001, over the course of which all the participating services judged the core reporting as "reliable." [One of the other services] recently affirmed that view—although the [service] ha[s] declined to provide details of sources who might provide corroboration.

Operational traffic . . . indicates the [hosting foreign service] may now be downgrading its own evaluation of the source's reliability.

It does not appear that this memorandum was circulated further; rather, the executive assistant explained that he would have used the memorandum to brief the DDCI at their daily staff meeting.

Former DDCI McLaughlin, however, said that he did not remember being apprised of this meeting. Mr. McLaughlin told the Commission that, although he remembered his executive assistant at some point making a passing reference to the effect that the executive assistant had heard about some issues with Curveball, he (Mr. McLaughlin) did not remember having ever been told in any specificity about the DO division's doubts about Curveball. Mr. McLaughlin added that, at the same time, he was receiving assurances from the relevant analysts to the effect that Curveball's information appeared good.

At about the same time, the division apparently tried another route to the top. Within a day or so after the December 19 meeting, the division's group chief said that she and the division chief met with James Pavitt (the Deputy Director for Operations) and Stephen Kappes (the Associate Deputy Director for Operations). At this meeting, according to the group chief, she repeated the Division's concerns about Curveball. But according to the group chief, Mr. Pavitt told her that she was not qualified to make a judgment about Curveball, and that judgments about Curveball should be made by analysts.

When asked about this meeting by Commission staff, Mr. Pavitt said that although he knew there were handling problems with Curveball, he did not recall any such meeting with the division chief or the group chief. Mr. Pavitt added, however, that he would have agreed that the call was one for the analysts to make. He also noted that he does not recall being aware, in December

2002, that Curveball was such a central source of information for the Intelligence Community's mobile BW judgments. For his part, Mr. Kappes does not specifically recall this meeting, although he said that the concerns about Curveball were generally known within the CIA. He also said that he did not become aware of the extensive reliance on Curveball until after the war.

That is where matters stood for about a month. But the issue arose once again in January 2003. During December and January, it became clear that the Secretary of State would be making an address on Iraq to the United Nations Security Council and that presenting American intelligence on Iraq's WMD programs would be a major part of the speech. In late January, the Secretary began "vetting" the intelligence in a series of long meetings at the CIA's Langley headquarters. In connection with those preparations, a copy of the speech was circulated so that various offices within CIA could check it for accuracy and ensure that material could be used without inappropriately disclosing sources and methods. As part of that process, the group chief received a copy. According to the group chief, she said that she "couldn't believe" the speech relied on Curveball's reporting, and immediately told the division chief about the situation. The group chief also said that she edited the language in a way that made the speech more appropriate.

According to the division chief, he was given the draft speech by an assistant, and he immediately redacted material based on Curveball's reporting. He then called the DDCI's executive assistant and asked to speak to the DDCI about the speech. When interviewed by Commission staff, the executive assistant did not recall having any such conversation with the division chief, nor did he remember seeing a redacted copy of the speech. However, another Directorate of Operations officer, who was responsible for evaluating the possible damage to DO sources from the release of information in the speech, remembers being approached during this time by the division chief. According to this officer, the division chief said he was concerned about the proposed inclusion of Curveball's information in the Powell speech and that the handling service itself thought Curveball was a "flake."

The DO officer responsible for sources and methods protection summarized these concerns in an electronic mail which he sent to another of the DDCI's aides for passage to the DDCI. The DO officer responsible for sources and methods did not recall that the division chief made any specific redactions of language from the draft. The DDCI's executive assistant has no recollection of such an electronic mail or of any concerns expressed about Curveball.

Later that afternoon, according to the division chief, he met with the DDCI to discuss the speech. The division chief recounted that he told the DDCI that there was a problem with the speech because it relied on information from Curveball, and that—based on his meeting with the foreign intelligence service representative—the division chief thought that Curveball could be a fabricator. Although the division chief told the Commission that he could not remember the DDCI's exact response, he got the impression that this was the first time that the DDCI had heard of a problem with Curveball. Specifically, the division chief recalled that the DDCI, on hearing that Curveball might be a fabricator, responded to the effect of: "Oh my! I hope that's not true." It was also at this time, according to the division chief, that he (the division chief) first learned that

Curveball provided the primary support for the Intelligence Community's judgments on BW.

The group chief provided indirect confirmation of the exchange; she remembered the division chief telling her about this exchange shortly after it occurred. Similarly, former DDO James Pavitt told the Commission that he remembered the division chief subsequently relating to him that the division chief had raised concerns about Curveball to the DDCI around the time of the Secretary of State's speech.

By contrast, former DDCI McLaughlin told the Commission that he did not remember any such meeting with the division chief. Specifically, the former DDCI said that he was not aware of the division chief contacting his (Mr. McLaughlin's) executive assistant to set up a meeting about Curveball; there was no such meeting on his official calendar; he could not recall ever talking to the division chief about Curveball; and he was not aware of any recommended redactions of sections of the draft speech based on Curveball's reporting. Moreover, Mr. McLaughlin told the Commission that the division chief never told him that Curveball might be a fabricator. The former DDCI added that it is inconceivable that he would have permitted information to be used in Secretary Powell's speech if reservations had been raised about it.

On January 24, 2003, the CIA sent another message to the CIA's relevant station asking for the foreign intelligence service's "transcripts of actual questions asked of, and response given by, Curveball concerning Iraq's BW program not later than . . . COB [close of business], 27 January 2003." The message further noted that the CIA had "learned that [the President] intend[ed] to refer to the Curveball information in a planned United Nations General Assembly (UNGA) speech on 29 January 2003." According to the division chief, this message was sent on behalf of the DCI's office, but was "released" by the group chief.

Three days later, on January 27, 2003, the relevant station responded and said that they were still attempting to obtain the transcripts. The message then noted:

> [The foreign liaison service handling Curveball] has not been able to verify his reporting. [This foreign service] has discussed Curveball with US [and others], but no one has been able to verify this information . . . .
>
> The source himself is problematical. Defer to headquarters but to use information from another liaison service's source whose information cannot be verified on such an important, key topic should take the most serious consideration.

Shortly after these messages were exchanged with the relevant station, the division chief told the DDCI's executive assistant that the foreign service would still not provide the CIA with access to Curveball. The division chief also sent an electronic mail—the text of which was prepared by the group chief—to the DDCI's executive assistant from the DO, which noted (in part):

> In response to your note, and in addition to your conversation with [the division chief], we have spoken with [the relevant] Station on Curve Ball:

- We are not certain that we know where Curve Ball is . . .
- Curve Ball has a history of being uncooperative. He is seeing the [handling foreign service soon] for more questions. The [handling foreign service] cannot move the meeting up, we have asked.
- [The foreign service] ha[s] agreed to our using the information publicly, but do[es] not want it sourced back to them. Neither the [foreign service] nor, per [the foreign service's] assessment, Curve Ball, will refute their information if it is made public and is not attributed. Per Station, and us, we should be careful to conceal the origin of the information since if Curve Ball is exposed, the family he left in Iraq will be killed.
- The [handling foreign service] cannot vouch for the validity of the information. They are concerned that he may not have had direct access, and that much of what he reported was not secret. (per WINPAC, the information they could corroborate was in open source literature or was imagery of locations that may not have been restricted.)
- [A magazine says that the handling foreign service has] intelligence information on the mobile poison capabilities of the Iraqis, but that they will not share it.

As a result, according to the division chief, the executive assistant told the division chief that the DDCI would speak to the analysts about the issue. Although the executive assistant did not remember such a conversation, former DDCI McLaughlin told the Commission that he remembered talking to the WINPAC BW analyst responsible for Iraq about Curveball in January or February 2003. Mr. McLaughlin said that he received strong assurances from the WINPAC analyst that the reporting was credible.

By this time, there was less than a week left before Secretary Powell's February 5 speech, and the vetting process was going full-bore. On February 3, 2003, the DDCI's executive assistant who had previously participated in meetings about Curveball sent a memorandum titled "[Foreign service] BW Source" to the division chief.

The memorandum, addressed to the division chief, read:

> [T]his will confirm the DDCI's informal request to touch base w/ the [relevant] stations once more on the current status/whereabouts of the émigré who reported on the mobile BW labs. A great deal of effort is being expended to vet the intelligence that underlies SecState's upcoming UN presentation. Similarly, we want to take every precaution against unwelcome surprises that might emerge concerning the intel case; clearly, public statements by this émigré, press accounts of his reporting or credibility, or even direct press access to him would cause a number of potential concerns. The DDCI would be grateful for the [Chief of Station's] view on the immediate "days-after" reaction in [the handling foreign service country] surrounding source of this key BW reporting.

Preparations for the United Nations address culminated with Secretary Powell, Director of Central Intelligence George Tenet, and support staff going to New York City prior to the speech, which was to be delivered on February 5, 2003. Until late in the night on February 4, Secretary Powell and Mr. Tenet continued to finalize aspects of the speech.

According to the division chief, at about midnight on the night before the speech, he was called at home by Mr. Tenet. As the division chief recalls the conversation, Mr. Tenet asked whether the division chief had a contact number for another foreign intelligence service (not the service handling Curveball) so Mr. Tenet could get clearance to use information from a source of that service. The division chief told the Commission that he took the opportunity to ask the DCI about the "[foreign service country] reporting" from the liaison service handling Curveball. Although he did not remember his exact words, the division chief says that he told Mr. Tenet something to the effect of "you know that the [foreign service] reporting has problems." According to the division chief, Mr. Tenet replied with words to the effect of "yeah, yeah," and that he was "exhausted." The division chief said that when he listened to the speech the next day, he was surprised that the information from Curveball had been included.

In contrast to the division chief's version of events, Mr. Tenet stated that while he had in fact called the division chief on the night before Secretary Powell's speech to obtain the telephone number (albeit in the early evening as opposed to midnight) there had been no discussion of Curveball or his reporting. Nor was there any indication that any information in the speech might be suspect. Mr. Tenet noted that it is inconceivable that he would have failed to raise with Secretary Powell any concerns about information in the speech about which Mr. Tenet had been made aware. Moreover, he noted that he had never been made aware of any concerns about Curveball until well after the cessation of major hostilities in Iraq.

In sum, there were concerns within the CIA—and most specifically the Directorate of Operations' division responsible for relations with the handling liaison service—about Curveball and his reporting. On several occasions, operations officers within this division expressed doubts about Curveball's credibility, the adequacy of his vetting, and the wisdom of relying so heavily on his information.

These views were expressed to CIA leadership, including at least the Associate Deputy Director for Operations and the executive assistant to the Deputy Director of Central Intelligence, and likely the Deputy Director for Operations and even—to some degree—mentioned to the Deputy Director of Central Intelligence himself. It would appear, however, that the criticism of Curveball grew less pointed when expressed in writing and as the issue rose through the CIA's chain of command. In other words, although we are confident that doubts about Curveball were expressed in one way or another to the Deputy Director for Central Intelligence, it is less clear whether those doubts were accompanied by the full, detailed panoply of information calling into question Curveball's reliability that was presented to more junior supervisors. We found no evidence that the doubts were conveyed by CIA leadership to policymakers in general—or Secretary Powell in particular.

As the discussion above illustrates, it is unclear precisely how and why these serious concerns about Curveball never reached Secretary Powell, despite his and his staff's vigorous efforts over several days in February 2003 to strip out every dubious piece of information in his proposed speech to the United Nations. It is clear, however, that serious concerns about Curveball were widely known at CIA in the months leading up to Secretary Powell's speech. In our view, the failure to convey these concerns to senior management, or, if such concerns were in fact raised to senior management, the failure to pass that information to Secretary Powell, represents a serious failure of management and leadership.

A team of Intelligence Community analysts was dispatched to Iraq in early summer 2003 to investigate the details of Iraq's BW program. The analysts were, in particular, investigating two trailers that had been discovered by Coalition forces in April and May 2003, which at the time were thought to be the mobile BW facilities described by Curveball. As the summer wore on, however, at least one WINPAC analyst who had traveled to Iraq, as well as some DIA and INR analysts, became increasingly doubtful that the trailers were BW-related.

The investigation also called into question other aspects of Curveball's reporting. According to one WINPAC BW analyst who was involved in the investigations, those individuals whom Curveball had identified as having been involved in the mobile BW program "all consistently denied knowing anything about this project." Furthermore, none of the supposed project designers even knew who Curveball was, which contradicted Curveball's claim that he had been involved with those individuals in developing the mobile BW program.

Additional research into Curveball's background in September 2003 revealed further discrepancies in his claims. For example, WINPAC analysts interviewed several of Curveball's supervisors at the government office where he had worked in Iraq. Curveball had claimed that this office had commenced a secret mobile BW program in 1995. But interviews with his supervisors, as well as friends and family members, confirmed that Curveball had been fired from his position in 1995. Moreover, one of Curveball's family members noted that he had been out of Iraq for substantial periods between 1995 and 1999, times during which Curveball had claimed he had been working on BW projects. In particular, Curveball claimed to have been present at the site of a BW production run when an accident occurred in 1998, killing twelve workers. But Curveball was not even in Iraq at that time, according to information supplied by family members and later confirmed by travel records.

By the end of October 2003, the WINPAC analysts conducting these investigations reported to the head of the ISG that they believed Curveball was a fabricator and that his reporting was "all false." But other WINPAC analysts, as well as CIA headquarters management, continued to support Curveball. By January 2004, however, when CIA obtained travel records confirming that Curveball had been out of Iraq during the time he claimed to have been working on the mobile BW program, most analysts became convinced that Curveball had fabricated his reporting.

Mr. Tenet was briefed on these findings on February 4, 2004. CIA management, however, was still reluctant to "go down the road" of admitting that Curveball was a fabricator. According to WINPAC analysts, CIA's DI management was slow in retreating from Curveball's information because of political concerns about how this would look to the "Seventh

Floor," the floor at Langley where CIA management have their offices, and to "downtown." CIA's Inspector General, in his post-war Inspection Report on WINPAC, concluded that "the process [of retreating from intelligence products derived from Curveball reporting] was drawn out principally due to three factors: (1) senior managers were determined to let the ISG in Iraq complete its work before correcting the mobile labs analysis; (2) the CIA was in the midst of trying to gain direct access to Curveball; and (3) WINPAC Biological and Chemical Group (BCG) management was struggling to reconcile strong differences among their BW analysts." Senior managers did not want to disavow Curveball only to find that his story stood up upon direct examination, or to find that "the ISG uncovered further evidence that would require additional adjustments to the story."

Any remaining doubts, however, were removed when the CIA was finally given access to Curveball himself in March 2004. At that time, Curveball's inability to explain discrepancies in his reporting, his description of facilities and events, and his general demeanor led to the conclusion that his information was unreliable. In particular, the CIA interviewers pressed Curveball to explain "discrepancies" between his aforementioned description of the site at Djerf al-Naddaf, which he had alleged was a key locus for transportable BW, and satellite imagery of the site which showed marked differences in layout from that which Curveball described.

Specifically, there was a six foot high wall that would have precluded mobile BW trailers from moving into and out of the facility as Curveball had claimed. Curveball was completely unable or unwilling to explain these discrepancies. The CIA concluded that Curveball had fabricated his reporting, and CIA and Defense HUMINT recalled all of it.

The CIA also hypothesized that Curveball was motivated to provide fabricated information by his desire to gain permanent asylum. Despite speculation that Curveball was encouraged to lie by the Iraqi National Congress (INC), the CIA's post-war investigations were unable to uncover any evidence that the INC or any other organization was directing Curveball to feed misleading information to the Intelligence Community.

Instead, the post-war investigations concluded that Curveball's reporting was not influenced by, controlled by, or connected to, the INC.

In fact, over all, CIA's post-war investigations revealed that INC-related sources had a minimal impact on pre-war assessments. The October 2002 NIE relied on reporting from two INC sources, both of whom were later deemed to be fabricators. One source—the INC source—provided fabricated reporting on the existence of mobile BW facilities in Iraq. The other source, whose information was provided in a text box in the NIE and sourced to a "defector," reported on the possible construction of a new nuclear facility in Iraq. The CIA concluded that this source was being "directed" by the INC to provide information to the U.S. Intelligence Community. Reporting from these two INC sources had a "negligible" impact on the overall assessments, however.

Another serious flaw affecting the Intelligence Community's pre-war assessments was its inability to keep reporting from a known fabricator out of finished intelligence. Specifically, the INC source, handled by DIA's Defense HUMINT Service, provided information on Iraqi mobile BW facilities that was initially thought to corroborate Curveball's reporting. The INC source was quickly deemed a fabricator in May 2002, however, and Defense HUMINT issued a fabrication notice but did not recall the reporting on mobile BW facilities in Iraq. Despite the fabrication notice, reporting from the INC source regarding Iraqi mobile BW facilities started to be used again several months later in finished intelligence—eventually ending up in the October 2002 NIE and in Secretary Powell's February 2003 speech to the United Nations Security Council.

This inability to prevent information known to be unreliable from making its way to policymakers was due to flawed processes at DIA's Defense HUMINT Service. Specifically, Defense HUMINT did not have in place a protocol to ensure that once a fabrication notice is issued, all previous reporting from that source is reissued with either a warning that the source might be a fabricator or a notice that the report is being recalled.

Though a fabrication notice was sent out, the reporting was never recalled, nor was the fabrication notice electronically attached to the original report. Analysts were thus forced to rely on their memory that a fabrication notice was issued for that source's reporting—a difficult task especially when they must be able to recognize that a particular report is from that source, which is not always obvious from the face of the report.

Some steps have been taken to remedy this procedural problem. First, DIA's Defense HUMINT Service has now taken steps to ensure that reporting from a fabricating source is reissued with either the fabrication notice or recall notice electronically attached, rather than simply issuing a fabrication notice. Second, the Director of the Central Intelligence Agency is currently working to establish Community-wide procedures to ensure that the information technology system links original reports, fabrication notices, and any subsequent recalls or corrections. Unfortunately, however, the Intelligence Community continues to lack a mechanism that electronically tracks the sources for finished intelligence materials or briefings. This makes "walking back" intelligence papers or briefings to policymakers difficult, as there is no way to know which pieces relied upon what information.

This failure properly to inform others that the INC source's reporting was not valid, however, was not merely a technical problem. DIA's Defense HUMINT Service also allowed Secretary Powell to use information from the INC source in his speech to the United Nations Security Council—even though a Defense HUMINT official was present at the coordination session at CIA held before the speech. A Defense HUMINT Division Chief, who was aware of the fabrication notice on the INC source, attended both of the February 2 and 3 coordination meetings for the Powell speech yet failed to alert the Secretary that one of the sources the speech relied upon was a fabricator. That Defense HUMINT official said that he was not aware that the information being discussed came from the INC source, indicating that Defense HUMINT had not adequately prepared itself for the meeting by reviewing the information Secretary Powell was considering using in the speech.

Conclusion

This section has revealed that Intelligence Community management was remiss in not taking action based on expressed concerns about Curveball's reliability. In retrospect, we conclude that the Intelligence Community's leadership should have more aggressively investigated Curveball's bona fides, rather than seeing the confidence of the analysts and the responsible liaison service as sufficient reason to dismiss the rival concerns of the operators and other liaison services. These leaders also should have pushed harder for access to Curveball—even at the cost of significant inter-liaison capital—given that the source's reporting was so critical to the judgment that Iraq was developing a mobile BW capability. After the NIE, CIA leadership should have paid closer heed to mounting concerns from the DO and, at the very least, informed senior policymakers about these concerns.

This said, the Community's failure to get the Iraq BW question right was not at its core the result of these managerial shortcomings. We need more and better human intelligence, but all such sources are inherently uncertain. Even if there had not been—as there was—affirmative reason to doubt Curveball's reporting, it is questionable whether such a broad conclusion (that Iraq had an active biological weapons production capability) should have been based almost entirely on the evidence of a single source to whom the U.S. Intelligence Community had never gained access. The Intelligence Community's failure to get the BW question right stemmed, first and foremost, from the strong prevailing assumptions about Iraq's intentions and behavior that led the Intelligence Community to conclude that Curveball's reporting was sufficient evidence to judge with "high confidence" that Iraq's offensive BW program was active and more advanced than it had been before the first Gulf War. The Intelligence Community placed too much weight on one source to whom the Community lacked direct access—

and did so without making clear to policymakers the extent of the judgment's reliance on this single, unvetted source.

The Commission also made the following "Biological Warfare Findings" in this section:

1. The DIA's Defense HUMINT Service's failure even to attempt to validate Curveball's reporting was a major failure in operation tradecraft.

2. Indications of possible problems with Curveball began to emerge well before the 2002 NIE. These early indications of problems—which suggested unstable behavior more than a lack of credibility— were discounted by the analysts working the Iraq WMD account. But given these warning signs, analysts should have viewed Curveball's information with greater skepticism and should have conveyed this skepticism in the NIE. The analysts' resistance to any information that could undermine Curveball's reliability suggests that the analysts were unduly wedded to a source that supported their assumptions about Iraq's BW programs.

3. The October 2002 NIE failed to communicate adequately to policymakers both the Community's near-total reliance on Curveball for its BW judgments, and the serious problems that characterized Curveball as a source.

4. Beginning in late 2002, some operations officers within the regional division of the CIA's Directorate of Operations that was responsible for relations with the liaison service handling Curveball

expressed serious concerns about Curveball's reliability to senior officials at the CIA, but these views were either (1) not thought to outweigh analytic assessments that Curveball's information was reliable or (2) disregarded because of managers' assessments that those views were not sufficiently convincing to warrant further elevation.

5. CIA management stood by Curveball's reporting long after post-war investigators in Iraq had established that he was lying about crucial issues.

6. In addition to the problems with Curveball, the Intelligence Community—and, particularly, the Defense HUMINT Service—failed to keep reporting from a known fabricator out of finished intelligence on Iraq's BW program in 2002 and 2003.

——

In August 2006, an interesting postscript appeared on the subject of the mobile biological weapons laboratories described by Curveball.

Steven Aftergood, author of an e-mail newsletter called "Secrecy News," which is published under the auspices of the Federation of Atomic Scientists' Project on Government Secrecy, picked up on a study done by Milton Leitenberg, a long-time expert on chemical, biological, and nuclear weapons at the University of Maryland.

He examined a single, crucial line in a memo in the Silberman-Robb report,* included above, in which the office of John

*www.wmd.gov/report.

275

McLaughlin, Tenet's deputy, reported that Curveball was judged credible for reasons including: *"Confirmation/replication of the described design by U.S. contractors (it works)."*

Leitenberg concluded there was no replication of the laboratories. "No mock-up containing the pieces of equipment shown in the drawings appears to have been produced, and no biological agent or simulant was produced," he wrote.

He concluded that the only drawings ever prepared were the ones used in Secretary Powell's presentation before the war, which can be read in full at http://www.whitehouse.gov/news/releases/2003/02/20030205-1.html.

"These self-conceived and self-imagined illustrations were all the 'evidence' that the United States government had to give to Secretary of State Powell to place before the United Nations and the world to support the claim that Iraq had mobile biological weapon production platforms," he added.

He also examined a second sentence, this one written after the report's release by McLaughlin and released to the public. It said that the processes Curveball described "had been assessed by an independent laboratory as workable engineering designs."

Leitenberg concluded that the illustrations of three vehicles meant to portray the biological weapons capability in Powell's presentation were produced by graphic artists under a CIA contract.

He said the drawings were not based on the descriptions of Curveball, rather on specifications made by CIA staff and the contractor on what equipment the vehicle would need. The drawings ended up in Powell's presentation and in a daily briefing for the president, Leitenberg wrote. He said the drawings were all that was produced and appeared to have been what McLaughlin was referring to in the second statement. Leitenberg concluded that a more accurate statement would be not that "the processes" had been validated, rather that an illustration had been made of the configuration of equipment that the CIA and its contractor—named by Leitenberg as Battelle—had deemed necessary for the task of producing biological weapons agents on truck platforms.

He decided that the phrase in the memo—"it works"—was evidence of overenthusiastic and/or careless language and it still referred to the drawings rather than some simulated weapons lab.

—

As my co-author and I prepared finally to go to publication, we sat down in the lobby of a hotel outside Washington to catch up and exchange thoughts about the latest news.

There was plenty to talk about. Israeli soldiers and Hezbollah militants were at war. The administration was portraying the eruption of violence as another front in the campaign against terrorism. But to Tyler, it was far more complicated than that.

"One thing to watch out for is that we don't make the war on terrorism into a self-fulfilling prophecy," he said. "Iraq has drawn young Muslims from Europe and other places to come and fight what they now see as their ultimate enemy.

"You end up with the same situation, on a grander scale, that you had with old communist terrorists."

For him, after 9/11, the administration dealt itself an even more difficult hand by beginning a war that has exacerbated divisions in the Arab world, pitting Sunnis and Shiites against each other and separately, against the United States. In his view, it has replaced one bipolar war—the Cold War—with another, only this one is with thousands of non-state actors spread around the world with whom the United States really cannot negotiate and who continue to exist even after their leaders are captured or eliminated. The administration, he fears, has set itself up for failure, and lumping Hezbollah so simply into the same pot as Al Qaeda only made it easier to turn a blind eye to the looming military failure being faced by Israel.

And if Hezbollah was not particularly focused on the question of the American presence in the Muslim world, as Al Qaeda followers so obsessively are, perhaps it was now, so his thinking was going that morning.

"Since 9/11, the situation in the Middle East is now completely different," he said. "It was always a dangerous, unstable part of the world but now there's a large American army occupying an Islamic country. The Sunnis see it as an American army protecting the Shia and vice versa and being there, you become a ping-pong ball between different factions who all see the American army as representing Israel's interests. It changes the whole dynamic."

Something else happened that morning that confirmed his view of the post-9/11 world.

The British government revealed details of a plot hatched by Britons of Pakistani origins to blow up airplanes bound for the United States. The news sent a shiver down my spine. But for Tyler, it was just more evidence of what he already believed—that terrorist cells were lurking in European communities waiting to be unearthed, as they had been during the Cold War, and as he was sure they could be again, if his government and those of its allies kept their cool.

I was reminded again that for him, and for many of his friends in the world of espionage, the war in Iraq was a distraction from the real business of pinning down and eliminating Al Qaeda supporters whose ranks, we were hearing increasingly, were swelling rather than diminishing as might have been anticipated after nearly five years of the War on Terror.

Rather than seeing the problem of Al Qaeda–inspired terrorism as a global battle between the forces of good and evil, he sees it as a struggle with individuals inspired by an ideology that in many ways, filled a void at the end of the Cold War. It has also, to at least some of his generation of intelligence professionals, inspired a type of thinking in the administration that reminds him of one of the most disastrous—and influential—episodes in American foreign policy: the Vietnam War.

"In Washington, everything old is new," he said as he reflected on the news from the Middle East and London.

The references by the administration to winning the hearts and minds of people in the Middle East, and using moderate mullahs to get the U.S. message out, and the diplomatic attempts to "sell" the U.S. image to populations unhappy with its foreign policies in the region, were a reminder of the days when the United States dreamed of winning hearts and minds in Vietnam. He scoffed at the idea that these mullahs would somehow go out and convince the extremists around them that "America is okay." Nor could Karen Hughes, appointed Under Secretary of State for Public Diplomacy and Public Affairs, fix the problem using her current strategy, he said.

"It's much deeper and more complex than that. It can't really be solved militarily—certainly not by sending Karen Hughes to talk to Saudi women about getting drivers' licenses." Soon after

Hughes assumed the role, she raised the issue of the kingdom's ban on women driving during a week-long tour of the Middle East to try to improve relations with the United States. Her point seemed not to find fertile ground. Critics suggested she missed an opportunity by addressing her point to a group of hand-selected, elite Saudi women who on the whole were probably quite able to live with the fact that someone else was paid to drive them wherever they wanted.

Tyler suddenly recalled the case of Wolfgang Grams, a Cold War terrorist from Germany. A court ruled that the forty-year-old Red Army Faction leader had taken his own life following a shootout that pitted him and his lover and like-minded militant Birgit Hogefeld, who is now serving a life sentence, against police officers. Police ambushed them at a railway station in the small town of Bad Kleinen in the former East Germany after they sat sipping milky coffee at a café, as Grams did every morning.

"Now *that's* a terrorist," Tyler said. "He never stopped fighting. I think that's what you're talking about with Al Qaeda." For him, while Al Qaeda uses far more dramatic methods to make its point, it is no more possible to negotiate with or defeat militarily the Islamic extremists than it was the left-wing terrorists who declared war on capitalism and U.S. imperialism. So there is no choice but to go after its members individually; for all the difference in scale and impact between the two movements, the work of the intelligence community and law enforcement in general should be no different. Doing anything else would be giving in to fear and playing into the hands of Osama bin Laden, he feels.

There is nothing particularly comforting in this view, though listening to Tyler, it is easier to live with than the notion of a clash of two worlds in which the United States must succeed, certainly given the success rate so far. Tyler's view accepts the notion that sometimes, attacks will succeed. But it also does not seek to create the false impression that the United States can wipe out Al Qaeda with bombs from the air and bullets on the ground. The Red Army Faction gave up fighting when they were ready, not because they had been obliterated in a battlefield somewhere.

I think his opposition to the Iraq war is driven primarily by the way it seemed to be declared in a vacuum; as if the problems that created the new terrorism only rose to the surface on 9/11. Ousting the Taliban in Afghanistan made sense because it was such an identifiable enemy, and Tyler believes the aftermath of that war would have led to more progress had the Iraq invasion not occurred the way it did. Before the war in Iraq, the Arab opponents of the United States, Britain and Israel—which they see as one amorphous mass—were mostly focused on the Israeli–Palestinian conflict. The first Afghan war, which pitted some of the same people, including bin Laden, against the forces of the Soviet Union, increased their confidence, he said. "These guys saw they could fight back against a major power. The legacy of that has spun out over the years, into the first Gulf War, which left American troops on the Arabian peninsula." Now Iraq has continued that tradition. If there were a "solution" to this type of terrorism, it would presuppose there was a solution the militants would accept, he said. That would mean the demise of Israel, which is not going to happen, he added.

By shunning traditional diplomacy in the Middle East in favor of the military option, the Bush administration, to Tyler, has also blunted a tool that is crucial to winning this war, if it can be called that.

The new terrorism is also a reflection of the irreversible march of globalization. He recalled how in the 1960s, he used to have to call the operator in Germany to get a line to the United States to talk to his grandparents, a far cry from now, where even people with limited access to cash and resources can travel and email and get their hands on modern high explosives, a tiny amount of which can do horrific damage to civilian targets.

This means sensible border controls and travel security, not hysterically keeping foreigners off American soil. It means "average people" being alert, he said, "so that if a bunch of Arabs come to your store and buy a ton of fertilizer and 50 gallons of fuel, maybe you should call someone."

He concluded with the thought: "In the end the only solution is just to put on your jersey every day and go play, because terrorism is always going to be there. If it's not this, it could be any group that feels it has no other options. It's the nature of the modern world."

ACKNOWLEDGMENTS

Tyler Drumheller

Several years ago, one of the legendary officers from the heyday of the Cold War told me that people have become cynical about the CIA, jaundiced by years of highly publicized scandals punctuated by vague and rather trite clichés about how our failures are publicized while our successes must remain secret. He knew that it had to be this way but said that the real tragedy lay in the fact that if people really knew what we had accomplished, their understanding of the history of the second half of the twentieth century and the beginning of the twenty-first century would be completely different. I would like to dedicate this book to the people of the clandestine service, both officers and families, who sacrificed lives of easy comfort to go out in the world to protect their fellow citizens. I list some of them below, but in truth they number in the thousands and they deserve to be recognized.

This book is the result of a lot of serious work by a group of good people without whose support we could not have brought forth the finished product. As always, I would have been totally lost without the support and participation of my wife, Linda, who has put up with all of my eccentricities for a long time, and keeps me focused when life gets complicated. While she never got the credit she deserved, we have always worked as a team and without her I would have been lost long ago. I also want to acknowledge the support and help of our daughter, Livia, who, after living her life in foreign lands surrounded by strange people, wanted nothing more than to finish her college career in peace, and ended up as a player in the dramatic events that led up to the war in Iraq. I cannot begin to express my thanks to Elaine, who put my ramblings together in readable English. None of this would have been possible without her talent, enthusiasm, and experience. By the same token, Joanna's hard work researching facts and checking details was invaluable and made certain that we got it right. And none of this would have happened if not for Danny and Carmen.

I also, for reasons they will understand, want to remember Mike, Steve, Ralph Oman, Ava, and Bill, along with Doug and the five chiefs who taught me the trade. I would also like to express my gratitude to Philip and everyone at Avalon. Finally, and most importantly, I have to acknowledge those absent friends who gave their lives for their country, particularly Mark, Debbie, Joao, W. E., Bob, and Mike. I hope this book serves their memories well.

Elaine Monaghan

My respect goes first to Tyler and his family, for their courage, spirit, and strength of character. Enough said.

Warm thanks also go to Danny, Bill, Ralph, and the boys.

I am indebted to: Carmen LaVia at Fifi Oscard Agency; everyone at Avalon, especially Philip Turner; Nina Graybill; and Peter Bale, Vanora Bennett, Lisa Dickey, Shamala Pietersz, and Rose Wild for reasons they will understand.

A grateful handshake to Mark Egan, and to Kate and Andrew for pardoning my absence at their wedding.

My mother, Margot, and sisters Bryony and Joanna helped in ways too numerous to mention, as did Paul. My brother Stuart also provided much moral support.

Finally, no words can express my gratitude to Lee for his love and endless support, and to Jack, the apple of my eye.

INDEX